UNDERSTANDING DEATH AND GRIEF

DAVE R. OESTER

ISBN-13: 978-1503156241
ISBN-10 1503156249

Edited by Dave R. Oester
Thesis by Sharon Gill Oester

Published by
Dave Oester, DD, PhD, Reiki Master
Coyote Moon Publishing
Kingman, AZ 86409 USA

Acknowledgments

The material for this book comes from the thesis my late wife, Sharon Gill Oester, did for her doctorate in metaphysical counseling with the university of metaphysics.

.

OTHER BOOKS
By Dave & Sharon Oester

The Prophecy
The Dark Wizard
Pandora Key
Hollow Earth
Lost Nazi Gold
Lost Aztec Gold
The Curse!
Ghost Riders Of The West
Ghostly Haunts Of The East
Gettysburg Ghosts
Tao Of Ghost Hunting
Beyond The Twilight
Beyond Death
Ghosts Of Gettysburg
Exploring The Haunted Southwest
Haunted Reality
Twilight Visitors
Living With Ghosts
Forbidden Knowledge
Ghost Hunting For Beginners
EVP Handbook
Ghost Photography Handbook
Magic Dimensions
Truth About Parallel Dimensions
How To Become A Reiki Master
How To Be A Ghost Researcher

How To Be A Paranormal Investigator
How To Be A Paranormal Counselor
How To Become An EVP Researcher
Ghostweb Journal
Magic Dimensions

Books By
Dave R. Oester

Awa Maru Treasure
Lost Egyptian Treasure
Noda, My Alien Spirt Guide
Internet Dating Scams
Lost Sun God Treasure
The Red Lake Mystery
The Rainbow Bridge

UNDERSTANDING DEATH AND GRIEF

DEATH

Death, is a subject that is spoken about as little as possible. It is seen as something that happens to other people, rather than ourselves. Most often, people speak of death only when they have lost a loved one to physical death or know someone who has lost a loved one. Only when death hits close to home, does the average person talk openly about it and question it. Yet the fact remains that every living thing eventually dies. Generally, people do not want to face their own mortality and by it being hidden in the background, we are denying that someday, we too will complete the cycle of this physical existence and pass on.

People, though they do not comprehend it, experience death in various forms, throughout their lifetimes. Death not only presents itself to us as the physical body ceasing to function, but also in ways that bring dramatic change to our lives. This is seen in the lives of most people existing all around us all of the time.

Death or a major ending or transition includes divorce, being fired from a job, bankruptcy, loss of a home, rape, the birth of a handicapped child, loss of childhood, leaving home or having children leave home. Abrupt changes or endings such as having a home collapse in an area of earthquakes, receiving a serious injury or having precious possessions stolen. It also includes gradual but definite changes in behavioral patterns; shifting out of a steady or an addictive relationship to a drug, a person, a behavior; outgrowing a stage of life, a philosophy, a religion or a cult; aging; having all your oldest friends die, or undergoing the disease process, be it temporary, chronic or terminal.

Also included is the model of death with which we think we are so familiar: physical death. Physical death, fear of it, avoidance of it, viewing it as final, is an excellent model for all deaths, small and great that each and every one of us must endure.

All deaths, no matter what type of death it is, can be endured. People can make it through any ordeal, no matter how impossible it seems at the time. It needs to be perceived as an opportunity, a new beginning, rather than as being a final chapter in our lives.

Death, is a loss of anything or anyone, that changes the direction of our lives. There is a dramatic emotional change for a period of time that must be dealt with for people to successfully heal and move forward. This is a critical time that most everyone of us faces at one time or another, in our lifetimes. It is crucial for people to come to an understanding of loss, the necessity of grieving and understanding this is a time of transition, of redirection and opportunity. Death is not the end, as perceived. It is a new beginning, not only for those who are left behind, as in the loss of a loved one, but also for those who have passed from this realm of existence.

At the age of 40, my life was everything I had ever dreamed it would be. I was happier than I could ever remember being. My husband and I were profoundly happy and in love. In 1986 we had moved from a place that we had found was in constant turmoil, to a place that offered new working conditions and opportunities. We found a beautiful home in the mountains, which we purchased and settled into. We were financially secure and it seemed everything was perfect in our new environment. We soon found ourselves living in a peace and harmony we had never experienced before. We had no idea how short our time together would be and there was no reason to think anything would change.

However, change did take place. It came unexpectedly and swiftly when my husband's heart exploded after a bout with pneumonia. At that point in time, my life would never again be the same, as death had taken someone very precious to me, bringing an end to the blissful existence we had known, together. This was just the beginning of what I came to term as, "the domino effect."

As the days passed, I was told I no longer had a job. Eight months later, I had to face the reality I could no longer keep my home. It seemed little by little, the life I had known and loved, was slipping away into something I no longer recognized or wanted. I had no comprehension as to why this was happening to me. The job market was tough to break into in the area. Friends and family had turned away from me. The world, through the eyes of a new widow, suddenly seemed very harsh and critical and I found myself very much alone.

My expectations of understanding from a religiously grounded family circle, brought me to the realization that even they were not able to deal with death, when it struck close to home. Every aspect of my life had changed, it wasn't just the spousal death I had to deal with, it was the total demise of my life I had to face. At a time when I needed companionship, love and understanding, I found there was no one there to help me through the grieving process.

I remember, clearly thinking how desperately wrong this was. It felt as though everyone saw death as a contagious disease and feared they would put themselves at risk by associating with me. I came to realize, people who had previously been an active part of my married life, had no idea how to deal with death or those who were experiencing the loss of a loved one. The reality of their own mortality was something my presence came to represent to them and it was more than they were able to deal with. They found it far easier to avoid an uncomfortable situation, thus, they backed away.

The most painful part of the whole scenario, was my family reacting in the manner of avoidance. I was raised in a very religious Evangelical Christian family, where accepting Jesus as Savior and involvement with the church, was an essential part of life. Accepting this tenet, assured an eternity in the realm of heaven, in eternal bliss. We were to accept death of those we loved, in joy, knowing our loved ones were by the side of Jesus.

Both my parents had been trained to arrange the memorial services in their church and frequently spent hours and days working with families to prepare the church according to their wishes, and the wishes of the deceased. My husband's sudden death was different, too close to their hearts for them to hear or to understand their daughters crises. Until this time, I never realized they could not face death, with understanding, on a personal level. I then began to question whether what they insisted to be truth, was something they truly did not believe. Since they found no comfort in their beliefs, they therefore were unable to give comfort to someone, like their daughter, suffering through such a loss.

Their faith was not sufficient enough to give them the strength they needed to remain by my side, in love and understanding. It was far easier to stay in the background and go about their lives in a normal way, shutting out the tragedy that had occurred. If we can't find love, compassion and understanding within our own family, where can we find the emotional support we so desperately need at such a tender time in our lives?

I involved myself with activities in the church I was attending at that time. I was thankful to have a church where I could learn, spiritually grow and give of myself in various ways. Yet after several months, I began to notice a change in the atmosphere there, as well. Not having a permanent job, I was able to volunteer to help with different activities in the church, where there was a need. When they expressed a need for help, I was able to volunteer my time. All I could give, was the free time I had available to me until I found full-time work. It was a blessing to me as it kept me busy and filled a need at the church.

I felt I was doing the right thing, giving of myself to help others. It soon became apparent, that all was not as it seemed, as the atmosphere in the church changed from warm and welcoming to cold. I left the church after a year, as it became a painful place to be. It was two years after I had moved from the area, returning for a short visit, that I was told, the Pastor of this place of worship had lustful intentions toward me. It seemed his way of dealing with those feelings, was to inform members of the congregation that the lustful intentions were mine, thus causing the word to spread like wildfire. I was the only one who remained uninformed as to what was taking place.

I not only had to deal with "the domino effect" in my life, I had to face the reality of abandonment and now betrayal. No one, should ever have to face that kind of pain. Those who knew me, understood, I was not the type of person the pastor alleged me to be. It came to light that what happened to me, had happened before and has happened since I left.

Within the church setting, even the Pastor was unable to deal with the loss sustained by a church member. His capacity was limited to his own human weaknesses that rendered him useless in working with the grief of a young widow. Again, I saw myself redirected due to tremendous change, and knew the church was inept in dealing with survivors of loss of that magnitude. I knew, deep in my soul, work needed to be done with those suffering loss, but I had no clue as to the direction my life would take.

I came to the point of discovery when I realized my strength to survive did not come from external sources but rather from within myself. The more experience I had with the obvious ignorance I saw in friends, family and in the church, the more I came to realize how desperately people needed to understand death and the grieving process. My greatest prayer, throughout the harshness of the life I had suddenly been thrown into, was that the experience would not leave me with a hard heart. I did not want to be embittered by it all, but I wanted to somehow use the knowledge I gained, to help others who would certainly, be in the same position.

The church experience, had fallen short of meeting the needs I had at the worst time of my life. It had, in fact, enhanced the feeling of loss extending the grieving process. It brought me to a place of courage to leave the beliefs I had known my whole life, to search for understanding and answers. It opened up a new world of opportunity and transition into a new phase of understanding life and the afterlife. I wish only to help others who find themselves alone and afraid after losing a loved one to understand and discover the truths I have found.

As I began work on my Doctoral Thesis, I was excited at the thought of earning the respected title of Ph.D. As I delved further into the documentation on the subject I had chosen, I realized my inadequacies in the field of death and loss. I felt as I pursued it for the sake of completing the project, I had far more to learn and experience.

For me, it is deeply important to fully earn what it is I wish to achieve. I had carefully selected the program offered by the University of Metaphysics so that I would have an opportunity to learn and grow in areas of which I had little understanding. I elected to work toward my PhD. rather than buy a degree to hang on my wall. I always would have regarded it as just a printed piece of paper.

As I worked through the Ministerial and Masters Degree phases of the course, I found something profound and meaningful. Something I could not only apply to my life but reach out to others who were seeking meaning and a better understanding of their own spirituality. I had grown to a position in which I was able to apply, and teach others. In discovering the spiritual side of life, I also came to know more about the spiritual side of death.

The past year has given me the experience I needed to feel confident in finishing the work on my Doctoral Thesis. I have found myself in positions to work with those so despondent with their lives they considered suicide to be their only answer. They were able to work through their negative thinking and the problems they had felt were impossible challenges and go on to find life's rewards, on their own. In a year's time I have seen more heartache, hardship and tragedy than I experienced ten years ago, after my husband died. So much a part of people's lives are a form of death, such as the loss of a job, loss of a spouse, moving from friends and family to start over someplace new and strange loss of faith. People sustain many kinds of loss, but have no understanding of the feelings of grief that result.

Most prominent this past year, have been the loss of friendships, family connections and friends who have lost children to cancer, which is the greatest loss of all. Having experienced the loss of my own spouse, ten years ago, I have a deeper understanding of the grieving process and the importance of enduring those feelings of grief.

Being a Metaphysician, I have had the ability to reach out and help those people understand the confusing, conglomerate of emotions that has taken over their lives and walk with them through their darkest hours. Knowing that grief from the loss of a loved one is a dreadful time that we all face at some time in our lives and being able to help them to a better understanding, has enriched my own life.

Background

The amount of documentation available on the subject of death is expanding as research into the subject becomes more popular within the scientific community.

Ten years ago, when I sought information for personal use, finding books on the subject that could help me endure such troubling times, were very difficult to find. In my research for this project I have discovered a multitude of references, from all different perspectives. The common denominator throughout all of the material I referenced was that we need to have a better understanding of the process of death and grief. There is no reason to fear our passing from this life into the next, if we come to view it as transition and acknowledge the value.

Our present approach in dealing with death is important in that our religious backgrounds effect our views. My research lead me to one such reference, Beyond Deaths Door, by Dr. Maurice Rawlings, MD., that discusses death and religion back through history from the Egyptian beliefs from 2500 B.C. through the scriptures we reference today. The Egyptian Book of the Dead, perhaps the first record written for guidance into the next life, considered death as, "an interruption in life, not it's end."

Our Christian views of today parallel the ancient views only we now find, "the missing link of the Creators revelation of Himself to His Creation in the form of man." With the personal Savior born in human form, whom we call Jesus, the belief about death changed. Dr. Rawlings explains that "Death is defined as a preparation of the body and the soul, but these two entities are eventually reunited at the resurrection. God the Creator of the soul, provides only one way of redemption through Jesus Christ."

We learn by the use of our five physical senses so we are limited as to our awareness. We still consider ourselves enlightened in all directions, yet the Bible, Matthew 13:13 tells us, "because seeing, they do not see and hearing they do not hear, nor do they understand."

The modern day American culture tends to shun the subject of death. We fear death because we fear what we do not understand. We place our confidence in beliefs that are interpreted by men of the cloth, but so often, they fear death themselves and are inept in handling care and comfort for the survivors of loss to death.

Loss of a loved one is the beginning of a life changing event for the survivors. The process of grief that ensues is emotionally dramatic, needing far greater understanding. Through volumes of grief related material, I found one book in particular, Companion through the Darkness, by

Stephanie Ericsson (1993:8) that described almost to the letter, my own experience in loss. Describing the feelings after losing a loved one is very difficult indeed, yet Ericsson adeptly expresses grief clearly, from her own devastating loss.

Being able to read, in someone else words, what you are feeling, is important in that you realize the experience is part of a universal process, not exclusive to you. You are assured you aren't losing your mind, and as crazy as it seems, your experience is normal. This gives great comfort in the time of turmoil and upheaval. According to Stephanie Ericsson, when talking of grief, she says, "It kills. Maims and cripples. It is the ashes from which the phoenix rises, and the mettle of birth. It returns life to the living dead. It teaches that there is nothing absolutely true or untrue. It assures the living that we know nothing for certain. It humbles. It shrouds. It blackens. It enlightens. Grief will make a new person out of you, if it doesn't kill you in the making."

This book was an excellent reference for not only research for this project but also for anyone facing the grief of loss. It reinforced every thought I had during my own experience of loss and encouraged me to focus more on the tremendous need we have for metaphysically oriented grief practitioners to enlighten and share higher knowledge of death and the process of grief.

One of the greatest pioneers in the study and work in the field of dying and death, is Dr. Elisabeth Kubler-Ross, MD. In her book, On Life After Death, (1997:10) she says we have chosen as a society not to discuss death, we ignore our own mortality which results in our not knowing what to do when we face the loss of someone we love.

If people spent half of the time understanding death as a natural part of life and what the process of grief involves rather than running from the thought, we would have an easier time of acceptance when death comes to someone close to us. We search for external answers to problems that must be dealt with internally. Grief is exclusive to our own emotional levels. In dealing with grief, we can expect to feel anger, guilt, hate, loneliness and internal conflict toward God on extreme levels. By understanding that these feelings are normal and must be confronted to heal, we can find it easier to endure.

Everything we face in life, hardships and trials that require our full attention, serve a purpose that has positive qualities for opportunities and growth. If we don't learn to listen to the inner voice deep within ourselves, we will not see the value in what we are given in this life.

Having gained much knowledge in all of her years of research, Dr. Kubler-Ross has many books available on the subject of death and working with the dying. Another book which I used closely as reference was Living with Death and Dying, is filled with valuable information regarding every aspect of death and the survivors of death. Dr. Kubler-Ross discusses the clergy and the difficulty some of them have in dealing with death. ". . .many members of the clergy are very uncomfortable and frightened in the face of sudden and violent death, too." After many years of working with dying patients she has seen the ineptness the clergy demonstrates. "Some ministers have little or no training along these lines at all," Dr. Kubler-Ross explains.

We expect our clergy to have the right words and the ability to console above all else, but this is not always the case. When this occurs, our religious beliefs fall short of our expectations and we feel betrayed and abandoned.

Since fear is always synonymous with loss, I felt it important to learn more about the origin of our fears. We fear what we do not know. Our fears are programmed into us from our childhood. Our lives are centered around and focused on the things in our lives that give us comfort and happiness. We avoid what we fear and those fears remain unresolved.

In, Embracing Death, by Angela Browne-Miller we are clearly told of our fears of change. Fear comes to us in two ways: one of help and one of hindrance to survival. "Fear used well serves a purpose. It can be a protective awareness, a survival instinct. Fear that is not used well, a fear that clouds consciousness is blind fear. Understanding the difference and recognizing that protective awareness is purposeful fear, blind fear can be harmful, is valuable especially when embarking into transition, due to traumatic changes or death."

Ms. Browne-Miller feels, as stated in her book, that we attempt to control our future lives by buying insurance, preparing a will, even praying for direction or salvation, yet we don't face our own mortality, we avoid it. Her book brings a far greater understanding to the ways we are programmed to deal with life and the effect it has on us.

To further understand fear and the impact it has on us in life, I referenced, Legacy of the Heart, The Spiritual Advantages of a Painful Childhood, by Dwayne Muller. Mr. Muller tells us that "When we are afraid, we lose our ability to feel our own inner strength and things precious and vital within us are smothered by our anxieties." Mr. Muller refers to what Hohandas Ghandi said, "Where there is fear, we lose the way of our spirit."

In his book, Mr. Muller elaborates on the reasons we turn to faith in something greater than ourselves. One major reason is to overcome our fears. This could be a part of understanding why our faith fails us when tragedy and loss come suddenly into our lives when it is our faith that should sustain us through anything we experience.

Though we hear the word, 'soul', used in many contexts, we truly have little understanding of the soul. The soul is the essence of who we are that transcends physical death. Care of the Soul, by Thomas Moore is one of the most excellent references regarding the soul and it's needs in life, that I have found in all of my research.

Thomas Moore takes a long hard look at the soul and understanding it. We need to take the time, through prayer or meditation to connect with our inner, deeper selves, or our souls. Organized religion does not teach us to know or understand the depth of the essence of who we are. Most everything around us is geared toward materialistic value, not the value we can find within us if we would only take the time to come to a deeper awareness.

Grief due to loss takes us to the place we normally tend to ignore, to the depths of our inner selves. In grief we must acknowledge our souls to come to an understanding of what is taking place. A survivor of loss to death is transformed into someone unrecognizable even to themselves. The transformation changes the person experiencing it and changes their paths in life. To endure these catastrophic changes, we must understand them and accept them. Survivors of loss are never again the same people they were before.

Depression is a big part of the grief process. Thomas Moore provides a new way of looking at depression and the role it plays in our emotional lives. Moore presents a profound and very different way of looking at what has always been considered a mental illness. Depression is an opportunity to look deep within at the more negative feelings, actually arising from the depths of our souls. Another opportunity we are given to acknowledge the soul and it's needs.

Thomas Moore discusses religion and faith in relationship to the soul. Religion is never neutral, being influential and strong. Religion is for the living, promoting beliefs in someone far greater than ourselves. We are taught that we can find all our needs met by prayerfully asking for the gifts of peace and comfort from God above in the Christian faith. In loss, the survivor finds that the comfort, peace and endurance, come from within. Survivors also learn it is a time of depending on their own inner strength, not on someone or something outside of themselves. It is a time of strengthening and learning, as I have experienced myself.

In faith, there must be an element of uncertainty with the certainty of faith or else we will fall victim to neurotic excesses to include superiority, vengefulness and cynicisms, as described by Thomas Moore. When our faith fails us in times of need, we fall into hopelessness and despair. Moore believes that anyone can turn to religion or spiritual practice as a means of escaping the hardships in life. The views expressed in Care of the Soul are applicable particularly when suffering a loss to death, and gaining strength and understanding of the essence of who we truly are.

In Experiencing the Soul, Eliot Jay Rosen discusses in depth, documentation of the soul surpassing death. The scriptures speak in terms of our soul living on after our physical body dies. The book is comprised of chapters written by various authors and philosophers contributing findings, opinions and theories regarding life after death. The book contains information regarding the effect of Near Death Experiences and the research into this phenomenon.

Part of this book reveals the value of Meditation and by implementing it into our lives we can experience the gaining of knowledge of life after death ourselves. We can gain knowledge of life on other planes of existence, without dying. In writing this document on life, death, grieving and helping others, I understand we are more than just physical beings. I felt the information in this book was an asset to this project. We can experience the realm beyond without experiencing a Near Death Experience.

Living through Personal Crisis, by Harmon Hartzell Bro, PhD., and June Avis Bro, D. Min., (1978) is a book on Edgar Cayce's wisdom for the new age. Using his psychic skills, Edgar Cayce revealed a wealth of information to help people work through crisis in their lives. We can learn how to cope, understand the deluge of emotions therefore, acknowledging the importance of accepting them and working through the steps necessary to heal.

Cayce explains the important role dreams play in helping us recover and heal from the crisis of loss. We can then take the knowledge we gain from our experiences and become agents of change, helping others to survive and heal.

The insights given relate fully to the other references used in this project and to my personal beliefs. Cayce' knowledge of the afterlife is extensive and helpful, to those suffering loss of a loved one.

One half of all Americans today claim to have had contact with someone who has died. Many of these contacts have come in the form of dreams.

To understand the analysis of dreams I consulted the work of C. G. Jung, translated by R.F.C. Hull, Dreams. (1974) According to Sigmund Freud, "Dreaming has meaning, like everything else we do." (1974:3) Dreams aren't just meaningless escapes we experience in sleep, from the busy, stressful, daily lives we lead.

Dreams have meaning, giving information, answering questions, giving peace to those who mourn. Dream states incorporate balance into our psychological processes. Dreams have a psychic structure and do not seem to be a part of our conscious psychic life. Dreams come in direct contrast to our conscious thinking.

Numerous accounts of contact with deceased loved ones have been documented since Biblical times. My own experience of contact lead me to, After Death Communication: Final Farewell, by Louis E. LeGrand, PhD.

Communication through dreams, visions, feeling, smelling, hearing and other unexplainable means is not uncommon. These contact help us heal in our grief and help the spirit of the deceased communicate messages necessary for them to move on. By understanding these are not hallucinations or mental disorders, we can accept that our souls live on and progress through the grieving process finding peace in that knowledge.

Dr. LeGrand expands on the importance of dreams, grief, healing and helping others through times of loss. The information given in this book was vital to this project.

The Metaphysical knowledge I have gained in combination with professionals working in the areas of loss and grief are an asset to helping society understand the complexities of life, by understanding death and loss.

If we come to know the truth about life after physical death, we can overcome fears that limit our thinking and actions only to discover our lives are richer and fuller from the knowledge.

The Metaphysical Funeral Ceremony in Rites of the Metaphysical Ministry by Dr. Paul Leon Master (1978) reinforces the subject of transcending physical death into a spiritual plane of existence through the wisdom expressed in the ceremony.

GRIEF

The process of grief is extremely complex and misunderstood. In our society death and grief are not spoken about because we fear our own morality. When death and loss occurs, there is no concept of what is happening or how to deal with it. Our Clergy fails in this regard because of having fears of their own. They are as mortal as anyone else. With the application of metaphysical principles in counseling, life changes become more acceptable. When people sustaining loss are made aware of this natural process as being transitional and made aware that everything that constitutes their pain is normal, they can begin to take the first steps down the path of healing.

Constituents of Loss

Loss comes into our lives in many ways. Bereavement is a time of feeling dispossessed or robbed of something belonging to oneself.

Loss of a loved one, spouse or family member is devastating and lives change because of it, never to be the same again. The surgical removal of a body part is taking a possession, serious illness that demands a change in ones lifestyle and work, is taking away choices and decisions of that person. Divorce, miscarriage, abortion or the inability to bear children are losses in their own right.

Situations that give one a sense of irrevocable injury, such as rape, chronic illness, birth of a defective child, job loss, career change, loss of a dream or goal, loss of personal possessions due to theft, fire or flood, a major move in which one leaves family and friends behind and the ultimate dispossession, the loss of ones own life.

Other forms of loss involve the loss of childhood due to an alcoholic parent, mental illness of a parent, influences of drugs and abusiveness or a broken family. In some way, life involves almost all of us in significant loss. It is at these times we come face to face with how fragile and vulnerable we are, something we would prefer not to confront.

Grief is not a mental illness, though it feels that way at times. The feelings of anxiety, fear, anger, sleeplessness, lack of interest, withdrawal, sensitivity to people and their words, profound sadness and focus on self and self-consciousness are not only symptomatic of mental illness but also constitute the grieving process. They are a natural part of grief. When realizing that life around you goes on as normal, one experiencing grief from loss, feels like they are on the brink of insanity. Try as one might, these feelings go on and on, and it feels like it will never end.

It is only much later when looking back to the time of the pain of loss, that we can clearly see how richly we have been transformed. We have walked the path of self-discovery, the catalyst to this has been, crisis.

At the onset and during the grief, we are at an all-time low in the way we feel and perceive life all around us. At that time, we cannot see what lies ahead, if anything. At the time of loss, everything is a reminder of what or who has been lost to us. Therefore everything intensifies the pain we feel and the preoccupation of the loss. We feel totally alone and isolated from the normal lives outside of us and feel alienated and suddenly foreign and unwanted in a world we were much a big part of not so long ago. We withdraw, as if into a darkened closet of our own despair, the pain inside is raging and relentless.

On top of all this seeming insanity, we begin to feel pulled and torn as people around us want us to get over it and step back into the mainstream of activity. The grieving process is one very much misunderstood in our society. There is no set time for a person to grieve, especially when a loved one has died very suddenly and unexpectedly. The lack of understanding can bring on feelings of self-doubt, anxiousness and fear in those suffering loss.

Grief is actually a very personal time of healing, of desensitizing ourselves to places, people and things that have been constant reminders of our loss. The process is long, difficult and necessary for complete healing and self-growth. There is no reason to fear the inwardness we feel, it is time necessary for us to recover and rebuild.

Loss brings change to us and the lives we have known. The structure of our joy and fulfillment does not die, we will find as time goes by, our joy and fulfillment comes to us in different ways. Loss also brings opportunities we never imagined. We discover an inner strength we never before knew existed and wisdom that can only come from surviving loss of intense magnitude. Almost as a Near-death Experience (NDE) brings great wisdom and life change, so does loss bring wisdom and change. Surviving grief can bring great insights into life around us. We come to understand more clearly, how very fragile life is and how mortal we are, as humans.

Understanding death and loss can bring us to a greater understanding of life and how precious it is. By allowing the process of grief to be a tool of education, we can clearly see the spiritual beings we truly are and the Universal connection in all intelligent life. The need for understanding and reaching out to others can become clear, if we allow ourselves to learn from the experience. Those around us, familiar or unfamiliar to us, have desperate need of love, understanding, compassion and human contact with those who have walked the path they now walk. My own experience has dictated, clearly, the need exists, to be there to comfort and guide.

Societal Views on Death

When loss comes suddenly, unexpectedly, one feels like they also are losing their minds. The loss of someone dear to us, is also a loss of our dreams and this loss rearranges and reprioritizes our lives. We feel small in the shadow of the ultimate truth that nothing in this life is absolute and can be taken from us in the twinkling of an eye.

Life, for the survivor, resembles something that has been dumped out of a shopping bag, and has landed randomly, all over the floor. It is a confusion what portion of the contents should be picked up first, as decisions become that difficult to make. Where life has been planned and organized accordingly; appointments books, calendars, notes to ourselves serve to remind us of our full days, we suddenly see our routines as unorganized conglomerates that are moving in slow motion. Like jigsaw puzzle pieces all around us, we have no idea where to begin picking them up.

We, as humans, work best within the organized structures we have developed for ourselves. Everything on our lists and schedules holds a place of importance that pertains to us, and to those close to us. In society today, we see this structure as a composition of who we are and what we value. Losing a spouse, or family member to death, our job, financial security, our health, any life altering event that puts those schedules, notes and appointments into meaningless, pieces of trash. Our lives, suddenly, no longer have the structure or organization, rather, we feel totally helpless, lacking direction of any kind. We can't think, making decisions is next to impossible, life feels like it is spiraling downward, out of control. This is the time, we need the people around us to be there and to help us make some sense of all this.

This is a time in our lives when we begin to recognize the lack of knowledge people have, regarding death. This much they do know, it is a painful experience they would prefer not to participate in. As helpful as they might like to be, what happens is, they find themselves at a loss for words. Suddenly, they are full of condescending advice.

Friends and family expect us, in our grief, to hold in the anger, the bitterness and refrain from speaking of our experience, and the depth of our sorrow. They want everything to be all better, right now. Their thinking dictates it is time to get over it and get on with life. They tell us they know how we feel, yet have never had the life altering experience we find ourselves in the middle of. They express how sorry they are for our loss, but what they want most is for everything to be as it was before the event. This is a normal human reaction, the avoidance of something people do not want to deal with and do not understand. The seeming cruelty is not intentional, yet it feels as though you are in the wrong place.

The loving, understanding friends you have known and hung around with for years, suddenly don't resemble the people you thought you knew so well. Overall, even the closest friends and family members, do not know how to deal with the loss of a spouse or loved one, nor the grief process itself.

How are you? Those around us care, automatically asking but not wanting to know, they are caught between sympathy and the fear, realizing this could happen to them too, not ready to accept it. "How are you?" has become a term of greeting rather than an inquiry for most people. But to greet someone bereaved, stirs an anger within them that becomes hard to suppress. The natural, common response is, "I'm fine," because that is what people really want to hear. But inside, someone grieving a loss, is no where near fine and won't be for quite some time. Grief of loss, is a long, hard, tedious journey along a path that leads to a new life. Not a life we know or recognize, but a life intended to be ours once the suffering eases and the lessons are learned. The process of grief is a process of awakening if we acknowledge it, learn from it and allow ourselves to grow from it in every aspect of the experience.

What our friends and family do not realize, is that after sustaining a significant loss, we are not the same people we once were. Our lives have been changed forever and for them to expect us to emerge from something of this magnitude, unscathed and the same, is ludicrous. Our lives change and along with it, we change, in every aspect of our being. The people we once were, have died with our loss, and we will never be the same again. We look at the reality of life as something different than we once did. We have gained a knowledge that will never leave us, because it has been a lesson in pain. It is what we do with this knowledge, that becomes the focus of importance.

Grief is defined as the act of accepting forced change. It is something that crashes down upon you with a force that is greater than can be described, tossing you around like a feather in a hurricane, ultimately throwing you out into an unknown place, battered, bruised and confused.

Suddenly there is little ability to concentrate or comprehend. Days drag into nights that slowly drag into more unrecognizable days. The rational mind is flattened by utter loneliness and you feel like an alien in a world that once filled you with joy and comfort. Friends back away as though suddenly facing the black plague as the brutal words of truth replace the soft-spoken tactfulness that was once related to who you were. Other people's problems and concerns suddenly appear as less than important and the sympathy you once shared freely appears more cynical.

According to Stephanie Ericsson, "Grief discriminates against no one. It kills. Maims and cripples. It is the ashes from which the phoenix rises, and the mettle of rebirth. It returns life to the living dead. It teaches that there is nothing absolutely true or untrue. It assures the living that we know nothing for certain. It humbles. It shrouds. It blackens. It enlightens. Grief will make a new person out of you, if it doesn't kill you in the making."

There are deep emotional feelings of despair, disappointment, revenge, retaliation, hopelessness, helplessness, diminished self-worth, nagging questions of why and what went wrong as well as fears of the future that accompany broken relationships and loss of position. "We who grieve are exiled in our society," says Ericsson. "Exiled by the lack of recognition of this universal experience."

Our culture teaches us that grief should be contained and not shared. Therefore, grief is most likely the most misunderstood process of them all. Yet everyone experiences grief in their lifetimes.

Grief is a gateway, a healthy path through tragedy that brings needed change.

Life and grief are inseparable. All relationships end in loss and separation. "You cannot have a single thought in your head which is not instantaneously translated into a bodily sensation. Thus, grief affects our entire being," says Dr. Irving Oyle.

The grieving process is a long, hard road, that requires certain steps to be taken, throughout the process. Each step must be completed, for a healthy transition into a new life and personhood.

Grief is a specific process, rather than a simple frame of mind. It is a process to renewal, for a purpose of awakening to self-awareness. There are no guidelines to grief, no time frames for the process, no correct way to grieve. Grief enfolds us in protective armor where we find ourselves confronted by the emotions that constitute the process.

Generally, grief is perceived as feelings of being overwhelmed by loss. What is less understood are the multiple moods within the grief process, that are normal and natural. Those suffering loss find themselves, face-to-face with intense emotions formerly experienced at a far lesser level, now emerging in a continuous flow from deep within themselves.

The feelings are as old as we are, they are familiar to us. They have been with us all along the way, but with the impact of loss, we now can clearly identify them, where before we have denied them, ignored them or repressed them. By acknowledging these feelings in times when our losses are smaller, which occur on a regular basis, we could prepare and not be overwhelmed, when a major loss, such as death, confronts us.

By coming into full awareness of our feelings, we may cultivate and prepare our hearts for greater, more intense feelings we all face in the future. Like exercising our physical bodies for strength, we can also exercise our mental faculties for emotional strength, by becoming aware of the need.

Our sadness, anger, frustrations and anxieties can be acknowledged, confronted and dealt with as they arise, rather than repressing or hiding them, excusing them as irrelevant, unnecessary or ridiculous. Too often, we find it easier to ignore the cause, so we shove them aside from our conscious thinking. They gather in a place of suppression and when sustaining a major loss, as in death of a loved one, they are released, fully and intensified, where we have to confront them, each of them.

The pain we feel at the time of loss, is the accumulated pain of a lifetime. These include feelings of doubt, fear and desperation that before loss, we have always withdrawn from. They become a full-blown part of our reality at times of loss.

Understanding Grief

Having people around us who are real helpers, along with dear friends and relatives, or professionals, can help us through the beginning stages of the grief process, making a big difference in coping. Too many crises at once, can stagger even the stoutest heart, but having people around to help get through the initial shock, gives us the strength to face the days.

As the victims of loss, we need the strength of those around us to depend upon. One factor to consider here is the style of dependency. To depend and lean on others for support is one thing, to live through others, is a very destructive means of coping in crisis. It is important to have people to lean on, who have an understanding of what is taking place, but they also must be people who can allow the grieving person, to be an active part of making decisions to help themselves through this time.

Unfortunately, at the time of the physical death of a loved one, there are a lot of decisions that have to be made. Those around us, can help with the decision making, but not take over completely, doing it for us.

Helpers, need to be there for us, to share in the experience. The ultimate experience, is still our own. Edgar Cayce felt that actively shared faith, a spiritual path, not just holding onto dogmas or obeying rituals and codes, can substantially cut the time of suffering, by as much as half.

Faith should not be used to deny the pain, the injustice or the loneliness of a bitter crisis. But this is one major way that the people around us can be of a positive help to us. It is a means by which we are internally strengthened, which is what we have to depend upon, through trying times.

Crisis agitates the psyche to a point that we fear we may never have the capacity to think clearly again. The mind in crisis never seems to silence itself. Our mental faculties seem to have run amok, thinking and decision making is difficult to the point of seeming impossible. Emotions are running rampant in a muddle of confusion and are inseparable. Sleep comes only with great difficulty and is interrupted when it does come to us, only compounding the problem.

In reference book after reference book, it is clearly indicated that in times of crisis, we strike out and blame God. We feel stripped naked and vulnerable and blame the God who, we are told, prevents these hardships, intervenes, if you will, should our faith be strong enough. When blaming God, one can find no comfort or peace in God or the religion we have been faithful to, prior to the crisis. We blame ourselves. The rage turns inward resulting in guilt and remorse. But coping requires gentleness with ourselves and understanding that the crisis is far greater than ourselves. At the time we feel, singled out, wondering why this happened to us, what we have done wrong and the questions run and rerun through our minds as time goes by.

The soul, learns from suffering, though clarity to this comes far later when emotions begin to recede from the forefront of our thoughts. Gently taking hold of our own sadness, helps us past the destructiveness of our own thoughts, preventing aggressive reactions to our grief.

"All things growing proclaim cycles of setting forth and returning, death and rebirth," says Edgar

Cayce. "In nature, endings lead straight into beginnings. Nature keeps the ways of the eternal, as well, in unyielding mountains, unwearying waterfalls, unending sea horizons."

"When the loss is to death or desertion or betrayal, after real intimacy and joint creation, then an empty place, a kind of tunnel to nowhere, is left right in the middle of our chests, though only the discerning may notice it. When a marriage of any substance is ended, even for a good reason, in divorce, the loss has the weight of losing a child of the same age as the relationship," says Cayce.

Cayce also felt, "Something that had its own life is permanently lost. Patience, honesty, tenderness, steadfastness, gratitude - each such strand must eventually be woven into the individualized rope that is finally to guide the mind of any one of us, past the chasms of dread into the unknown that a crisis brings."

Prayer and Meditation project positive vibrational energies that return to us, vibrating into our cells and thoughts, breaking down the protective hardness, we may not even realize is there. By this process of breaking away the impenetrable hard shell, the healing, transforming energies we need, can get through. Resonance is a key process in prayer and meditation.

Edgar Cayce expressed that, "There is reason to suspect that crisis brings not only shock, but it's own internal medicines to heighten awareness of the ultimate." (1988:19) We are more able to touch the inner, more spiritual side of ourselves, because we are searching for answers. Unfortunately, it takes a crises for most, to come to the point of going within. It is then, we learn, the strengths come from deep within ourselves and we can learn to develop this spiritual awareness to depend upon, long after the crises has passed.

Once a person has passed the stages of coping and acceptance of grief, we need to look for answers to our situation, and we must expect a new growth in the person we are. Having been held within the cocoon of despair, we now find ourselves in the process of rebirth. We have been given the wings to fly in new ways. Part of such growth, is the gift of awakening under pressing demand.

We are at a point in our lives, where choices have not been a consideration, we are thrown into situations out of our control. Now we have to take what has been given to us, and walk the path before us into new and unfamiliar territory. What we do with the opportunity, is fully up to us.

Pity vs. Self-Pity

Self-pity, when losing a loved one is a personal right. It is natural when a significant loss is sustained to feel sorry for ourselves and for having to face a future, at least for a time, alone. The burden of survival has fully fallen on our shoulders and we are thrown into a world of singleness, a place where we never wanted to be again. We had found our comfort and joy, in the life we were sharing.

Pity from others, can be debilitating, while we are feeling self-pity. It is like being slapped in the face, when suddenly the people around you offer pity for the position you find yourself in. It is not a position of choice, in fact quite the contrary. Pity tends to mar our competence, our strength and our transformation.

With acceptance, the pity of others takes us down to levels where we start to manipulate to get what we want. Once the manipulating begins, if not caught and corrected, it becomes a habit. Using our grief to help us, is not a healthy habit to get caught up in. There are those who do not recognize it, for what it truly is.

When manipulating, our purpose then is to use outside pity, to benefit ourselves and it works well, when we allow it to enter into our consciousness. What we do not realize at the time, it also serves to separate us from others. This type of behavior is abusive to others and becomes transparent as to the purpose, after taking place for any length of time, causing resentment, thus incurring more loss and feelings of confusion and betrayal. For the completion of a normal grieving process, we need not accept the pity of others, but stand on our own two feet through the transition into a healthy, new life.

Manipulation enables us to become dependent on the strengths and assets of those around us. It binds us to co-dependency not allowing growth on a personal level. The experience of loss is a personal, strength-giving, spiritually-growing time, given for a higher purpose. It is either perceived as a punishment or an opportunity, depending on the individual. What the person does with what is available, after loss, is a personal decision as well.

Those who have taken the grieving process, step-by-step and have searched for greater knowledge, using it for growth, have discovered a keener awareness to all aspects of life. They find a greater meaning and purpose through loss, and what has been gained is essential to become the new people we are destined to be on a different path to new life.

There is also the element of pride in the success of overcoming hardship. We have an inner strength we never knew was within us and a courage to endure what has been dealt us. The strength and growth comes from depending on our own innate abilities, not retraining ourselves to manipulate and depend on others because of a tragic situation. Learning to use our hardships to manipulate, stifles the transition into growth and awareness. Pity can compound already existing self-pity, only if the survivor of loss, accepts it.

Death as a Natural Part of Life

"Dying is a human process in the same way that being born is a normal and all-human process" says Dr. Elisabeth Kubler-Ross. We, as a society have chosen not to talk about death, therefore, we do not know how to deal with it when it comes.

The greatest lesson in this life, that we all need to learn, is how to love, unconditionally. When this lesson is learned and practiced in life, we are free to return to the place, from where we came. "When your house burned down, when your child died, when your husband hurt himself, or when you yourself suffered a heart attack, all fatal blows were merely some of the many possibilities for you to grow: to grow in understanding , to grow in love, to grow in all those things which we still have to learn." says Dr. Ross. "We are created for a very simple, beautiful and wonderful life. My greatest wish is that you will start to look at life differently. If you accept your life as something you were created for, then you will no longer question whose lives should be extended and whose should not."

When we face all the hardships we are given in life, all the trials and tribulations, nightmares, impossible situations, losses, all the negative things that come to us, we see them as being punishment from God. But nothing negative comes to us that isn't, in actuality, positive in that the value of these experiences are given to help us to grow and gain wisdom. They should be seen as gifts, in the manner in which they are given. Gifts that enable us to listen to the voice deep within ourselves and touch the wisdom within us. By listening to the inner voice, we will find the answers to what we encounter, truly lie there. Sometimes it takes great turmoil to bring us to a place of silence, to seek our inner wisdom. It will not lead us the wrong way, if we listen.

"Get in touch with your own inner self and learn not to be afraid. One way to not be afraid is to know that death does not exist, that everything in this life has a positive purpose. Get rid of all your negativity and begin to view life as a challenge, a testing ground of your own inner resources and strength." Dr. Ross says.

You will be given an opportunity at the time of you own death - not to be judged by a judgmental God, but to judge yourself, by having to review every single action, every word and every thought of your life. You make your own hell or your own heaven by the way you have lived. After all, in our lives, we are usually our own worst critics. So it is also in death.

"Everyday people die all over the world. Yet in a society that is able to send a man to the moon and bring him back well and safe, we have never put any effort into the definition of human death," says Dr. Kubler-Ross. "The scriptures are full of symbolic language. If people would listen more to their own intuitive spiritual quadrant and not contaminate their understanding of these beautiful messages with their own negativity, their own fears, their own guilt, their own need to punish others or themselves they would begin to comprehend the beautiful, symbolic language that dying patients use when they try to convey to us their needs, their knowledge and their awareness."

FEAR

The Fears of Our Clergy

" . . .strange as it seems, many members of the clergy are very uncomfortable and frightened in the face of sudden and violent death too. They haven't had time to prepare themselves for sudden tragedy and in attempting to console, they may grope for words and may not find the right ones. Some ministers have little or no training along these lines at all." says Dr. Elisabeth Kubler-Ross, MD. "

It is the doctors task to break the news to the family and ministers who try to find the most comforting words are men with their own fears of death and. . .the unknown, and they are not as comfortable as we sometimes think they should be. The doctor or minister is a person with his own inability to cope with such things, the same as the rest of us and that's sometimes hard to remember." says Dr. Ross.

This response came as a result of a nurse overhearing a Priest consoling a family who had just lost a loved one by saying simply, it was God's will. This could imply to family members that the death was "Gods will so don't grieve and don't be angry.

Most people would respond with tremendous resentment of God and justifiably so!" Dr. Ross says. Dr. Elisabeth Kubler-Ross, having worked with dying patients for many years, feels people should come to terms with death before such things happen. Death is not God, as we tend to equate the two. Any more than the magic trick is the magician. Like birth or illness or old age, death is just another event along the way.

Understanding Our Fears of Death

There is a great paradox in dealing with the issue of death. To live our lives fully, we must come to terms with death and the fear of it. Our survival instinct gives root to our fear of death as it is the protective mechanism built into us as self-preservation.

Fear of death is not only built into our nervous systems, we are programmed into fight-or-flight. It is acquired by societal and parental learned programming. So from an early age, we are taught to be careful, to defend ourselves and we are warned about all of the horrible things that can happen if we aren't careful out in the big bad world. This inadvertently programs us into the fear of death, though it is so automatic, we think little of it.

This acquired fear can also stem from core beliefs that are unaccepting of free expression in life, as well. It becomes the inner script that is a conscious or unconscious factor that not only limits how we subjectively live life but also plays a role in the words, deeds and thoughts we have during our lifetimes here on earth. The fear of death will go with us to deaths door, if the issue is not examined, understood, and dealt with successfully.

The degree of discomfort we experience regarding the issue of death comes from how much we have been affected by the exposure we have had to societies negative views of death.

We hear misinformation on the dying process and ignore the evidence and testimonies that support redefining of death as transition, not the ending of life. Going into ourselves to discover the richness in our soul and experiencing it, holds the answers to letting go of this needless fear.

As the poet Rabindranath Tagore said, "Death is not the extinguishing of light; it is only the putting out the lamp because the dawn has come."

"When death is not the enemy, then clarity, generosity and courage become the way of life." Stephen Levin said, "Death puts life into perspective. A great gift which if received in love and wisdom allows the clinging mind to dissolve so that nothing remains but truth. And we become just the light entering the light."

Meditation brings us to a point of being mercifully aware to our deathbed situation, softening resistance to pain in the physical body. The willingness to work with the pain by means of meditation, going deep within, softens it. As we go deeper within ourselves, we discover layers of depth. As the physical body dies externally we find internally we are becoming freer.

Fear of the Darkness

What is it that creates such a fear within us that turns our thoughts away from the subject of death? Since our experience comes from our five physical senses we can only perceive death as darkness. I relate darkness to lack of knowledge. Religion teaches us to look at death in terms of black and white, God of Eternal Light or Satan, the Prince of Darkness. The second stirring fear in us as we fear the darkness and what we cannot see or understand.

In life, we seek to spend our daylight hours completing the tasks of the day, being inside the warmth of our well lit homes before the fall of darkness. We unconsciously center our active lives around the light of day, thinking little of it. We are creatures of habit, creatures of the light. Darkness stirs feelings of unease that whatever lurks in the darkness can only be of evil intent. Ghosts and monsters come to life in the darkness and we fear them. Or maybe it is the darkness within us we fear. Regardless, darkness is representative of fear of the unknown. What then, would better describe death than the fear of an eternity in darkness. Substantiated and instilled fully in us by organized religion.

Understanding Human Spirit

We can discuss the human spirit with wonder, as long as it is alive and well. But when discussion arises as to a human spirit, disembodied, our minds revert back to the dark ages way of thinking. We cannot conceive of the human spirit living on, outside of its translating into a realm we accept as being heaven. Anything outside of that, turns our thoughts to darkness, evil and menacing to the living. We are taught throughout our lives that anything of a paranormal nature, is evil and demonic.

People cannot think beyond their own realm of experience. We depend on what we have been taught to help us comprehend. Until recently, religious beliefs have been our only means by which we have learned about what happens after death. Scientific research has been limited greatly.

Humans are energy. Our minds and our thinking is energy on an electromagnetic energy level. We have scientific equipment that reads and records this process.

According to the second law of Thermodynamics, energy cannot be destroyed, only transformed. The idea of all life ending at death, is conflictive with the laws of Physics that we have proven to be true and correct. The scientific community is warily starting to re-evaluate their views of death.

The documented stories of Near-Death Experiences, have given indication that the spirit, or soul, leaves the body at physical death, but lives on with clarity of his/her surroundings. They find themselves fully awake, aware and alive without the anchor of a physical vessel that has broken down unable to sustain physical life.

Fear of Change

Death or a major ending or transition includes, divorce, being fired, leaving home, or having children leave home, abrupt changes or endings such as having a home collapse in an earthquake, receiving a serious injury or having precious possessions stolen. It also includes gradual but definite changes in behavioral patterns; shifting out of a steady or an addictive relationship to a drug, a person, a behavior; outgrowing a stage of life, a philosophy, a religion or a cult; aging; having all your oldest friends die; undergoing the disease process, be it temporary, chronic or terminal. Also included is the model of death with which we think we are so familiar: physical death. Physical death, fear of it, avoidance of it, viewing it as final, is an excellent model for all deaths, small and great that each and every one of us must endure.

All deaths can be endured. We can make it through any ordeal, no matter how impossible it seems. Nothing in this life is constant, there are changes taking place all around us on a daily basis. They may be subtle and easily accepted, as someone changing their mind about a lunch date or a vacation spot. These things take place everyday, everywhere. We find ourselves comfortable with the small changes and deal with them regularly. But a change that effects our lifestyles, our ways of thinking, when they strike close to us, are extremely difficult for us to accept and our first reaction is a natural question, "why is this happening to me?"

All changes in our comfortable ways of life, that we have become so accustomed to, are a death, of sort. When we cannot see death as anything other than just that, it is an extremely painful experience. If we can begin to view them outside of just being painful experiences, we can use them well. When using hindsight, which gives a full perspective on a past event, we can view traumatic experiences without the full emotion of that moment and actually see, it was necessary.

We can also see those events as being beneficial. It was a passage, a transition that led us down a different path to where we are presently. It can be viewed as a change that needed to take place, for without it, there would have been no growth into the person we have become. The death of anything or anyone is an ending of the old and a beginning of the new.

By understanding the process, the more you can use the death experience to consciously create the next phase of your life and being, to design your new reality. No death is the same and yet within the passage lie similar characteristics that when recognized, can make the journey challenging and remarkable, enriching the experience.

People fear changes, especially when those changes are not of their choosing, but are sudden, major and traumatic. Our attempt to control our future lives, is not by consciously facing our mortality, or our life's insecurities, but by buying insurance, writing a will and praying for some kind of salvation or direction.

"Fear is one of four mental conditions that keeps us from knowing how to plan for, manage, take control of, successfully endure, and harvest all our dying process. Next to fear is our deep programming, the behavioral and energetic patterning we are programmed to be addicted to. And next to pattern addiction is lack of information: we have not been taught the true nature of death.

We have either denied ourselves or have been denied the truth about our existence. And beyond these states of mind is the social state of mind - the cultural taboos and laws we have developed and enacted against learning how to die well, against actually dying a physical death with grace," says Angela Browne-Miller.

"To master death, whatever sort of death or transition being faced, we must see the difference between the two basic types of fear, one a help and one a hindrance to survival," Ms Browne-Miller tells us. Fear, used well serves a purpose. It can be a protective awareness, a survival instinct. Fear that is not used well, a fear that clouds consciousness is blind fear. Understanding the difference and recognizing that protective awareness is purposeful fear, blind fear can be harmful, is valuable especially when embarking into transition, due to traumatic changes or death.

Blind fear is all-consuming, inhibiting, it is an emotion that makes no allowance for change, for growth, for exploration outside of what is already comfortable within us. When we have a blind fear of loss, the struggle for survival is increased as acceptance of the new condition is resisted. It enhances our inability rather than allow us to recognize the new, strong abilities we have deep within us.

Blind fear makes transitions seem impossible to our perception and for us to come to a place of acceptance of the new role we have in life, it takes someone of specific training to guide us back to a place that is less fearful.

Knowledge, allows us to face our fears of the changes and as we deal with the upheaval of emotion and work through the grieving process, step-by-step, we can re-enter the mainstream of life, with renewed strength. Fear can be present within us, but does not have to be debilitating when entering transition. It is only with this knowledge that we can eliminate the blind fear and go slowly forward, facing life a day at a time, while readjusting to the new beginning we have been given.

Fear and Faith

"Since we are rarely in mortal danger, we may discover that most of our fears are generated by the mind," says Wayne Muller. Even though we are reasonably safe and cared for, we still go about our lives with fear and trembling. Why? Not because we fear the present but because we fear the future. We can seemingly handle what we are given today, but our expectations are that we will face more than we can bear in the future.

We can observe, in those around us, how pain of the past can create within us bitterness, anger and grief. "Just as grief arises in response to past pain, fear is our response to pain in the future," states Mr. Muller. We must learn to understand our fears and learn to heal what scares us. Exploring and understanding our fears can help us to overcome them. We can expand upon this understanding to bring ourselves beyond the frailties we feel in life, to having confidence and faith in our own strengths.

Faith has been used in religious traditions for so long, we relate faith to something greater than we, outside of ourselves. Faith is used as leverage, as to whether one can enter the kingdom of heaven or not. If you have enough faith in God, you become a child of God and will be granted your greatest desires.

Prayer and faith in the teachings of the church, when strong enough, can bring miracles that eliminate the fear and hardship in this life, easing the burdens we are given to carry. "An adequate supply of faith would assure us that all would turn out the way we hoped," Mr. Muller tells us.

Yet, if the truth be known, faith becomes a wedge between the faithful and the unfaithful. Many have been deeply hurt by those who felt driven by moral obligation to judge the spiritual worthiness of others, by taking measure of their faith. This is especially painful and abusive to those who are poor, struggle with serious illness are culturally different, where there appear to have been no miracles taking place to change things, faith is deemed to be weak or lacking.

This also applies to loss. When one loses a person, possessions, income, a child, anything I have discussed previously, there are those who will stand in judgment saying we have sinned against God, therefore, we are being punished for the wrong we have done. The word faith, as defined in religion, therefore begins to feel like a weapon of judgment used against us.

To reclaim faith for ourselves, we need to understand that faith is a way of being. "It is a place inside where we are in a compassionate relationship with what is strong and whole within ourselves, where we listen to the still, small voices of our heart and soul." says Muller. He goes on to tell us, "When we are practicing a path of faith, we are in intimate conversation with what is deepest in our mind, heart and spirit." Faith in ones strengths and abilities is essential to heal from the pains of loss.

A Buddhist teaching about equanimity is, "the ability to experience the changes in our lives, circumstances and feelings and still remain calm, centered and unmoved."

"Genuine faith is born of the ability to trust in what is most fundamentally true within ourselves," says Muller. (1993:27) Yet, this is not necessarily what we are taught to believe in mainstream religion today. Our lives continually change, we experience peaks and valleys, great joys and great sorrows.

But the purpose of faith is not to miraculously eliminate difficulties we encounter in our daily lives. "The real question of faith is when pain and loss inevitably come our way, do we withdraw in fear that we will be destroyed, or do we deepen our trust in our innate capacity to endure them? Faith is a centering response. The search for faith is a search for our true nature, for the spirit within, the divine strength that lives in our deepest heart."

"Unfortunately, many of us must be devastated by some tragic moment before we will reluctantly place our trust is what is deepest within ourselves. Many of us never imagine the depth of our inner strength until we find ourselves confronting a terminal illness, experiencing a divorce, or suffering the loss of a spouse, a friend or a child."

"Face-to-face with tragedy, illness or death, many of us actually become less fearful - not because life holds any less danger, but because in those moments we are propelled deep into ourselves, reaching to uncover what is strong, reliable and whole within our own hearts and spirits. Even in the midst of a personal hell, we discover within ourselves a heart of courage," Wayne Muller states.

I have found, for myself, this statement to be absolutely true. When facing a crisis, such a the loss of a spouse, you find yourself in a sink or swim situation. In many cases, the widow or widower left behind after the death of a spouse, passes away as well, unable to deal with the overwhelming sense of grief and loss. Be it to natural causes, such as a broken heart, or be it suicide to join the loved one on the other side, people find faith in God to be insufficient at such devastating times.

Rather than believing in the inner strength we all have to endure and rise above the pain and hardship, it is often easier, when feeling abandoned by our religious upbringing, to crumble beneath the weight of our sorrow. Mainstream religion tries to prepare us for what we will encounter on the other side, heaven or hell according to our conduct in life. Yet it does not prepare us, or give us knowledge of what to expect when we lose a part of our lives to death.

ILLNESS, FORGIVING AND HEALING

Illness, Forgiving and Healing

We are more responsible to our illnesses than we are for them. If you feel responsible for your illness, you suddenly find yourself backing away from it. This way of thinking causes guilt, fear and helplessness. This way of thinking is an anti-healing mindfulness, it blocks the healing processes that result in closing the heart.

Being responsible to the illness allows us to confront it, befriend it and embrace it. In this way you are able to send love, mercy and soften to yourself and others. You can then feel you deserve to heal rather than being judgmental and merciless.

To hear someone say, "God saved my child," when the child was near death, is sickening. Especially when you realize half a million other children have died from the same illness. That indicates that God has singled out one child because he was chosen of God. The difference is the changes within the heart of that person.

Illness doesn't come to us because of sins we have committed or something we have done wrong. Illness that can extract us from this physical life comes from biological changes and the breaking down of the physical body. Accepting this for what it truly is, increases our awareness of being mortal and makes the transition into death more merciful for us.

We need to forgive ourselves, which in turn may help someone else. Forgiving gives you access to your own heart, opening it up rather than closing it down.

Forgiveness takes away the barriers we've built up, that have kept people out. In forgiving ourselves and others, we eliminate barriers and anchors that having been torn down, frees our souls. Forgiveness heals not only us but those around us. The body may pass away but the soul has been given the freedom to soar. In learning to forgive ourselves in physical life, it comes easier to forgive ourselves as we panoramically review our life after death. In this manner, we are able to move on, not anchoring our spirits to this physical plane.

The Importance of Forgiveness

Pain and suffering are not synonymous. Pain is related to the reaction of nerve endings throughout the body. If you bump into something, the physical body responds in turn by aching, pain and discoloration. It is a physical reaction to outside stimulus.

It is the resistance to pain, not allowing it to come into our hearts that causes suffering. Suffering is deep within the mind and can be softened by integrating our minds confusions with a whole heart. The practice of forgiveness allows the act of letting go of the suffering that can anchor the soul to this lower plane of existence, after death.

The act of forgiveness is not one of condoning behavior that causes suffering in us. It is understanding that the persons heart does not yet see or understand, someone whose heart was closed. Forgiveness is given according to the crime, so to speak. To be physically tortured by someone is an extreme by which forgiveness will not come easily so it must come in degrees. Otherwise, the result may be it coming back to you in the manner of self-hatred and guilt. Be merciful to yourself, not allowing dire circumstances to give rise to the inability to forgive yourself.

Generally our true nature is one of light. When dark clouds of incidence block that light, allowing suffering to enter in and close our hearts, we need to recognize the problem and give ourselves permission to forgive the shadows, let them pass on and allow the light to shine brightly. We are allowing ourselves to go on, unabated.

Forgiveness is opening your heart to that which gives you greater access to your true nature, letting go of that which causes the suffering. Allow yourself to find the stillness within, leaving resentment and baggage outside.

SOUL

Carl Jung said that every psychological problem is ultimately a matter of religion. "A spiritual life is of some kind is absolutely necessary for psychological health; at the same time, excessive or ungrounded spirituality can also be dangerous leading to all kinds of compulsive and even violent behavior."

"Tradition teaches that the soul lies midway between understanding and unconsciousness, and that its instrument is neither the mind nor the body, but imagination. Fulfilling work, rewarding relationships, personal power and relief from symptoms are all gifts of the soul." Says Moore.

In this modern day and age we live in deep division. Mind is separate from the body and spirituality is at odds with materialism. Our attitudes are dualistic and we need to find a way out of this problem. Without realizing it, we can become fully absorbed into the materialistic way of life, forgetting our spirituality.

Our daily lives draw us into a yearning for entertainment, power, intimacy, sexual fulfillment and material things that we seek to find in the right job or relationship, the right church or the right therapy. We strive to gather these things to us in great masses, thinking quantity will satisfy our longings without thought of quality.

Caring for the soul, "speaks to the longings we feel and to the symptoms that drive us crazy, but it is not a path away from shadow or death," says Moore. "A soulful personality is complicated, multifaceted, and shaped by both pain and pleasure, success and failure. Life lived soulfully is not without moments of darkness and periods of foolishness. Dropping the salvation fantasy frees us up to the possibility of self-knowledge and self-acceptance, which are the very foundation of the soul"

When someone sustains the loss of a loved one, particularly a spouse, everything that was once held in a place of importance, fades into oblivion. The focus changes from what we have, to the reality of who we are. This brings me to the theory that at the time of loss, we unknowingly come face-to-face with the urgent needs of our own soul. We focus on our spirituality rather than our possessions. It is a turning point, a transition that when recognized, can lead us into harmony and balance within us. Life changes when we lose a spouse or loved one, not only life around us, but the spirit within us. Death of a loved one is soul-changing, literally. For months or years that we term as a period of grieving, we are actually brought to the place where our thoughts center on meeting the needs of our own soul. We discover our spiritual side which may have been set aside and dormant for many years as we built our materialistic kingdom in which to dwell with loved ones.

Our soul isn't something that cares for itself, it requires our attention. But we can complicate our lives to the point that our total focus is away from the care of our own souls. The less attention we give to our soul, the more we strive to fill our inner longings with "things" outside of our inner yearnings.

Yet we are never fully satisfied and the cycle is endless, working harder to gain more, outside of the real unacknowledged needs. More and more every day, we hear how people are seeking a spiritual need, searching for something outside of the modern, high-tech world we exist in. That need, is the care of our souls that is going unfulfilled and unrecognized in this day and age.

"Many of our words for psychological work have religious overtones. In Platos' writing, Socrates says that 'therapy' refers to service to the gods. A therapist, Socrates says, is a sacristan, someone who takes care of the practical elements in religious worship. Another phrase Plato used was heautou epimeleisthai, or 'care of oneself.' This word for care also described honoring the gods and the dead. Somehow we have to understand that we cannot solve our 'emotional' problems until we grasp this mystery that honoring the divine and the departed is part of the basic care that as human beings we have to bring to life." Thomas Moore states.

Soul is not the ego, but rather it is closely connected to fate. Fate almost always is contrary to our expectations and desires of the ego. "Care of the soul is not solving the puzzle of life; quite the opposite, it is an appreciation of the paradoxical mysteries that blend light and darkness into the grandeur of what human life and culture can be." Says Moore.

Joseph Campbell put a lot of emphasis on following a person's bliss. Since the soul requires the constant process of care, Campbell may actually have meant to follow your inner longings to hold on to the bliss that fills and attends to the yearnings of one's soul. This supports the soul and its care, resulting in bliss.

"Soul is not a thing, but a quality or dimension of experiencing life and ourselves. It has to do with depth, value, relatedness, heart and personal substance," Says Moore.

As humans, our basic intention of caring, be it physical or psychological, is to eliminate suffering. But most important in caring is the listening and looking carefully at the suffering being revealed.

In the Tao Te Ching, Chapter 64, it says, "He brings men back to what they have lost. He helps the ten thousand things find their own nature, but refrains from action." The importance here is to not take away the face of the problem but to face and accept it by befriending it. Making an enemy of it is equivalent to swimming against the tide, using vast amounts of energy with making little progress.

We tend to throw experiences into one of two categories; good oncs and bad ones. But looking closer, there can be value found in every experience, even those that feel negative and undesirable. This coincides with Jung's' theory of shadow. "One consists of the possibilities in life that we reject because of choices we have made. Such as, the person we choose to be creates the dark double - the person we choose not to be."

"When normalcy explodes or breaks out into craziness or shadow, we might look closely, before running for cover and before attempting to restore familiar order, at the potential meaningfulness of the event." This is especially true at times of loss, be it to physical death of a loved one, possessions, relationships or lifestyle.

An old Chinese Proverb tells us that when climbing stairs, each step is important, but to get to the next step you must go beyond, letting go of the step you are standing on. This wisdom applies perfectly to working through the process of grieving and becoming whole, once again.

Understanding The Soul

We need some silence and solitude in our lives to connect with our inner, deeper selves. With the conveniences of television, radio, stereos, computers, telephones, and other distractions in our lives, we find little time for the silence we need to listen to the subtle voice within each of us. It is easy to begin to see how we lose touch with ourselves and neglect the care of our souls.

We are so busy and so focused on connecting with the people and things around us, we don't take the time to develop that all important connection to our higher spiritual selves, the Soul within us. There is no doubt that people can be extremely religious, yet their actions depict values every day that are contrary to their Sunday beliefs. Churchgoing can become a mere aesthetic experience or, psychologically, even a defense against the power of the holy. Formal religion, so powerful and influential in the establishment of values and principles, always lie on the cusp between the divine and the demonic. Religion is never neutral. It justifies and inflames the emotions of a holy war, and fosters profound guilt about love and sex.

Growing old is one of the ways the soul nudges itself into attention to the spiritual aspect of life. Aging forces us to look at what is important in life. When taking the time to look at ourselves, our value and our lives, people tend to confuse self-understanding with rational analysis.

Aging into mid-life and older are commonly referred to as our "golden years" and we recognize this as a time to slow down and enjoy all the things around us that we weren't able to take time to do while busily raising our families and working to earn a living to support those families. As we slow down, we come to an awareness of ourselves through the time we have for reflection.

We reach for consciousness, awareness and the highest value in our spirituality. "In our soulfulness, we endure the most pleasurable and the most exhausting experiences and emotions." Says Moore. When facing life's greatest challenges, we need to recall Jung's warning about dealing with the present problems by wishing for a return to former conditions. Jung called this, "regressive restoration of persona." Meaning that we tend to attempt to restore what we imagine were better conditions of the past, we call the "good old days."

If we resist improving the present by regressing to the past, we can fully confront today's challenges.

We Have Lost Touch
With Our Inner Selves

"The key to lost spirituality and numbing materialism is not merely to intensify our quest for spirituality, but to re-imagine it," says Thomas Moore.

According to Ficino in the late 1400's, "The more compulsively materialistic we are, the more neurotic our spirituality becomes, and visa versa." Spirituality is not specifically religious, as many may think. The spirit takes us out of the confines of human dimensions, nourishing the needs of the soul. A long walk along the seashore, feeling the warm sun and soft breeze, gifts us feelings of peace deep within, nourishing the needs of the soul.

Jung equates the unconscious with the soul. "When we live fully consciously in an intellectually predictable world, protected from all mysteries and comfortable with conformity, we lose our everyday opportunities for a soulful life." The intellect wants to know, like the inquiring mind wants answers to it's questions and curiosities, while the soul requires the element of surprise to for fulfillment.

If we could come to the awareness that the simple idea that some of our actions do not have an effect on our actual lives, but rather go deeper touching the souls desires, we might give more to the soul everyday letting go of the dominant role of function, to reach a new wholeness. But first we need to realize how important this is to us.

Some cases of Psychosis and Neurosis often take form in compulsive rituals, or more commonly habits. Neurosis is the loss of imagination, where a person "acts out."

"It's easy to go crazy in the life of the spirit, warring against those who disagree, proselytizing for our own personal attachments rather than expressing our own soulfulness, or taking narcissistic satisfactions in our beliefs rather than finding meaning and pleasure in spirituality that is available to everyone."

Soul Meaning in Loneliness and Depression

"Loneliness is a major complaint and is responsible for deep seated emotional pain that leads to despair and a consideration of suicide" says Thomas Moore. Dealing with loneliness begins at the depth of the soul. Our soul is not neutral, it is the energy, the source of our lives, who we are.

If we do not acknowledge the soul and claim the energy therein, on our own behalf, we can, in turn becomes it's victims. We suffer from our emotions instead of just feel them working for us. We hold thoughts, desires and passions inside of ourselves allowing them to become disconnected from life, and that is what begins to stir the trouble within us. As a result, we begin to feel depressed, unsettled, restless and without dealing with these feelings that continue to gain strength, we become ill.

We consider depression in our society to be an enemy. A malady that progressively worsens and seemingly becomes unredeemable. Depression is actually a mood closer to our feelings of mortality. We are taught to deny death and yet depression is a normal part of the soul's cycles. We need to have a healthy respect for its' place as it enters and leaves our lives like an uninvited guest.

Sometimes, our strongest feelings and thoughts are with us when we experience a dark mood. Dark moods take us to a place of deeper thinking, away from the materialistic side of life. When the mood is suppressed, those ideas and reflections are suppressed as well. Depression may be a very important means by which we tap into more "negative" feelings, just as affection is an expression of love. The void and gloominess experienced in depression awakens and calls upon the awareness and articulation that is hidden behind the higher moods we all prefer to experience. Things that we suppress and refuse to acknowledge normally. The experience of depression, or melancholy, is opening the portal to the soul to reveal and express a side of its nature that is as valid and important as the high, happy moods we experience.

Depression grants the gift of experience, as an attitude rather than a literal fact. You come to realize that life is suffering, that wisdom makes the difference. Suppression of emotion is not using the wisdom that we are given to deal with our emotions.

We come to bouts of depression as a part of the aging process as well. Leaving youth behind leaves us with a sense of loss. By accepting the depression, we accept our own mortality. Since depression has the attached connotation of being bad, we deny depression as having value. But depression contributes valuable coagulation of thoughts and emotions, gathered into values and philosophy that gives substance and firmness to our lives from our experiences.

If we broaden our thoughts on depression, we find that "feelings of emptiness, loss of familiar understandings and structures in life, and the vanishing enthusiasm, even though they seem negative, are elements that can be appropriated and used to give life fresh imagination." says Dr. Moore.

We have this strange notion that our lives are to be monotheistic, always full of cheerfulness. As friends or counselors, we feel challenged when we encounter those who are depressed, wanting to draw them out of it. Instead we need to acknowledge this mood and look at it as a time to learn. Yet depression, as any emotion, can go beyond the normal limits to a point of being debilitating. Even then, it can be of value if we look deep within the core of it. Approaching depression at the onset and befriending it could, in fact, prevent it from extending into the far depths of illness. One anxiety associated with depression is that life will never find its' way back to joyfulness and activity.

As we stop fighting against the depression and begin to acknowledge it's lessons and go with the flow of it, this anxiety of entrapment decreases.

Periods of depression can bring about imagery of death at times. At times people feel their lives are over and hopes for a future are dashed, due to depression. The values and understandings they have lived with for years no longer make sense.

"Care of the soul requires acceptance of all this dying," Says Dr. Moore. Sensing that life is over, a positive, affirming approach might be a conscious, artful surrender to these emotions and thoughts that the state of depression has created.

Nicholas of Cusa, a Renaissance theologian, revealed through a vision, that "we should acknowledge our ignorance of the most profound things." (1994:142) If we seek to discover mysteries unknown to us, such as the meaning of life or who God is, we begin a more grounded, open-minded kind of knowledge that does not result in closed minds or fixed opinions.

With the onset of a state of depression, we often find emptiness in meaning in our lives, which indicates how attached we are to our ways of understanding and reason. We can have our thoughts and philosophies wrapped up in such a neat little package, we disallow new thinking in areas concerning the mysteries of life. This is a closed way of existing in a life where there are so many variables and so many questions without definite answers. When depression sets in, it leaves a void, or better yet a portal by which knowledge can be accessed if our efforts aren't directed at sealing the hole. This gap that appears with the state of depression, that throws doubt onto our ordered theories and opinions, can be used as a means of healing.

Learning our limits may not only be a conscious effort, our education may come to us in the form of depression. Our happiness ceases during depression to bring us to the state of mind to evaluate our knowledge, our thoughts and assumptions as well as our value and purpose in life. This rings true not only in temporary depression but in acute depression as well. We can re-evaluate our beliefs by which we have lived our lives, beginning to let go of the old and learning to reconstruct a new foundation on which to rebuild. Depression can be the soul crying out for the lack of care, demanding attention for necessary changes that we need to acknowledge and tend to.

We, as a society recognize the joyful and active side of life as being normal, and we are fully accepting of this and expect this in everyone involved with us. When a depressive condition comes into our being, we are unaccepting of this and the ultimate goal is to change this abnormal mood experience. When someone suffers the loss of someone dear to them, they go with the deep feelings and accept it as the process of grief. Those around them are not so accepting, as their lives haven't changed due to the loss, therefore they want the survivor of loss to return to their normal, joyous selves.

Such statements as, "get over it" are common, doing far more harm than good. I can see the Yin-Yang as something normal in our lives and should be regarded as just that, normal. Our lives are filled with opposites, Yin and Yang, our personal moods and feelings are no exception. Yet, society takes a dim view of depression and ignores the value that can be found within it.

The traditional process of treating depression, is by chemical means, called antidepressants. But a closer view shows us that chemical treatment, takes away from the process of caring for the soul and meeting its needs to discover our essential selves within the framework of the depression.

Though therapy, talking about the feelings, is incorporated into the full treatment of depression, we have found that it is not necessary to speak ones way through the painful experiences to find relief. Neurolinguistic Programming is another way of treating a person, without the aid of chemical relief. This process has been a successful means of treatment eliminating the threat of chemical dependence.

Accepting Death and
After Death Communication

Rather than going through life, shoving thoughts of our demise into the back of our minds, if we could just come to the realization that death, change and grief are normal conditions of life, and integral part of being human, it might be more acceptable to us. There are no exceptions, no one escapes those conditions.

Preparation and acceptance will limit, and in some cases eliminate unnecessary suffering. Education about death starts with adults who are willing to listen. The refusal to talk about death in an open manner and the refusal of so many of the bereaved to relate contact experiences when they occur is based on our fear. Not only the fear of death and what we will find on the other side of life, but fear of admitting there has been contact, by means of dreams or actual visual contact from a deceased loved one. The fear of being challenged and being called "crazy" stands out as one of the greatest fears we have. Yet these contacts do take place and they are unfamiliar, only because we do not speak of them. We can take charge of our own destiny by preparing for life's inevitable losses and accepting consciously that loss is a factor in life. Accepting death, is accepting life itself, and our lives can be fuller and richer in its acceptance.

The Soul After Death

Our soul is consciousness itself, a formless essence, much the same as the essence of God, the All-Consciousness or the Universal Consciousness. The soul is permanent and indestructible, having come from the Universal Consciousness, it also returns to the Universal Consciousness upon physical death.

Thanatology: Research Into
Near-Death Experiences and ADC

"Death is simply a shedding of the physical body like the butterfly shedding it's cocoon. It is a transition to a higher state of consciousness where you continue to perceive, to understand, to laugh and to be able to grow." According to Elisabeth Kubler-Ross, MD. Dr. Sigmund Freud became a member of the British Society for Psychical Research, becoming very impressed with the research. He said, "If I had my life to live over again, I would devote it to psychical research instead of psychoanalysis."

Dr. Wayne Dyer once said, "We are not human beings having a spiritual experience; we are spiritual beings having a human experience." The more research that is done in the field of Thanatology, the more we are finding there is far more to the human soul than meets the eye.

After shedding the physical body, our existence continues. We continue on to another plane of consciousness at a higher vibrational rate that requires no physical body. The essence of who we are; our personality, emotions, intelligence, those things that, when combined, create the spirit of our personage. Those who have gone before us, live on.

After the death of a loved one, we may find ourselves receiving some form of communication from them. After Death Communications are as old as mankind itself and have been reported from cultures all over the world. It gives people great peace to know there is an afterlife. Those who have Near-death Experiences return to find their lives totally changed. Much research is being done into this phenomenon. Near-death Experiences may be new to the scientific community, but we can find references to them throughout our history, involving great saints and mystics who discuss sojourning into the beyond. They describe the spiritual realm as being filled with love and beauty.

Guru Nanak in the JapJi wrote: Sach Khand, or the Realm of Truth, is the seat of the Formless One, He creates all creation, rejoicing in creating. Here are many regions, heavenly systems and universes, to count which were to count the countless. Here, out of the Formless, the heavenly plateaus and all else come into form, all destined to move according to His Will. He who is blessed with this vision, rejoices in its contemplation, but O'Nanak, such is its beauty that try to describe it is to attempt the impossible.

Previously, discussions on the afterlife were centered around a religious belief. People hesitate to discuss their Near-death Experiences for fear of being labeled "crazy." Science, and medical professionals started documenting these cases and discovered there were too many people having NDE's to dismiss the evidence. The similarities in the cases being documented were startling that surpassed nationality, religion and social backgrounds.

NEAR DEATH EXPERIENCES

Near Death Experiences

Many people who have experienced clinical death tell us of actually seeing themselves, separated from their physical bodies, into spirit form. They can see and hear people in the room with their lifeless body yet they cannot be seen or heard by them. We view the person who has died as fully gone. The Bible says much about the body aging and decaying, returning to dust from which it came. But the spirit lives on.

Death is startlingly real. It is the respecter of no man. Reprieve cannot be bought, it cannot be earned as each of us will face deaths door. If we find no meaning in this life, we will find the same in death. Religion teaches us far more about life, than of death. By coming to a clearer understanding of life, we find we become more accepting of death.

Physical death is a fact of life. Dying patients need no longer be the neglected patient. The dying need the closeness and sympathy of someone who can relate to him. We all will end up facing our own physical demise and should consider that we also could be the neglected dying patient or one who is still surrounded by those we love and those things we love. Vast amounts of literature have come from those studying the dying patient. Dr. Karlis Osis, Dr. Erlendur Haraldson, Dr. Phillip Swihart and Dr. Elisabeth Kubler-Ross are just to name a few of the great leaders researching the death experience.

In Near-Death Experiences, those returning to share the afterlife experience found the focal point of the experience to be: learning to love others and gaining wisdom while on this earth plane. The bond of love surpasses the grave as I have found in the research I have done.

We learn by experience. Religion is taught and we take on faith the lessons taught from man's interpretation of scripture. We are taught to fear, yet to find hope in salvation. Subconsciously we learn that death is the end, the path to a dark void. This seems to be the message of our experience.

The Role of Faith

". . .we are a people afraid of the heights to which the spirit might take us and so we turn to forms of religion that temper and contain the spirit that potentially could transform our lives. We go to church as much to subdue that spirit as to acknowledge it." say Thomas Moore.

"Faith is a gift of the spirit that allows the soul to remain attached to its own unfolding. When faith is soulful it is planted in the soil of wonder and questioning. It isn't a defensive and anxious holding on to certain objects of belief because doubt, as it's shadow, can be brought into a faith that is fully mature." says Moore.

Many people tend to put their faith into spiritual leaders raising them high on a pedestal of godliness. I have seen this occur frequently throughout my life, within my own immediate family. When the ideals we expect these men to uphold, fall short and they demonstrate their humanness, we feel betrayed and disillusioned. It is a real trust of faith to understand from the start that life and personality are not without shadows and betrayal is inevitable. Soul faith contains two elements, the believer and the disbeliever, or skeptic. When questions come to mind bringing doubt, drifting away from a time from commitments, changes in the understanding of one's faith may seem like weakness. But to the soul these feelings are necessary in creating the shadow that actually strengthens faith that fills it out and rids it of perfectionism. Again, I refer to the Yin-Yang, to the balance necessary in all things. The Angel of belief and the Devil of doubt in regard to faith.

There must be an element of uncertainty with the certainty in faith, else wise we can fall victim to neurotic excesses to include feelings of superiority, vengeful of those who betrayed us or cynical about trusting anyone. If faith doesn't include an element of doubt, we can split away from ourselves and our souls to become embodied and identified with others. When this happens, we feel as though we cannot trust others outside of those we identify with. Living only the positive side of faith can bring paranoid suspicion of others and in the changes we all experience in our physical lives.

By not accepting the shadowy side of our faith, our faith focuses on the romance and the fantasy of our beliefs. There are those whose beliefs are absolute, believing it to be the whole life. They have no trust in anything or anyone outside of their belief systems and their affiliation. A belief can be fixed and unchanging but faith is almost always in the presence of an Angel.

It is always easy to maintain a firm, absolute belief and faith in religious tenets when life remains on a smooth, unaltered path. But when the path suddenly becomes one of hardship and suffering with things out of our control, faith begins to falter and leave us, leading to hopelessness and despair. The true feelings of peacefulness, when our faith in religious teachings fails us in crisis, can be found deep within when connecting with the soul. Our suffering takes us to the deep recesses of ourselves that we would normally ignore. A lesson taught by many mystics is, "that the necessary dimension of faith is spawned by unknowing." By not educating our ignorance we keep the full presence of the divine at bay. We have to come to the point of not knowing what is happening or what to do as it is at this point we find the portal to true faith.

Fundamentalism verses Polytheism

"Often, when spirituality loses its soul, it takes on the shadow form of fundamentalism." Said Moore. No particular group or sect, "but to a point of view that can seize any of us about anything."

Moore defines fundamentalism as "a defense against the overtones of life, the richness and polytheism of imagination." Where fundamentalism tends to narrow down and give definition and romance to a story, at the same time, it takes the mystery from a sacred story, robbing it of its soul. It takes away our own ability to define and develop our own moral values. "The tragedy of fundamentalism in any context is its capacity to freeze life into a solid cube of meaning."

To refer to the Bible for moral certainty, proof of faith or for avoidance of doubt and the anxiety of making difficult choices in life, is totally different than looking to it for insights. The Bible is something to believe in for the Fundamentalist. For the soul, the Bible stimulates religious imagination, for searching the heart for its deepest and most exalted possibilities. When spirituality loses contact with soul, it can become rigid, simplistic, moralistic and authoritarian - qualities that demonstrate the loss of soul.

"The intellect often demands proof that it is on solid ground. The thought of the soul finds its grounding in a different way. It likes persuasion, subtle analysis, an inner logic and elegance. It enjoys the kind of discussion that is never complete, that ends with a desire for further talk or reading. It is content with uncertainty and wonder. Soul knows the relativity of its claim on truth." says Moore. The soul seeks insights more than truth, and subjectivity and imagination are always in play.

Exploring further, Moore goes on to explain, "Truth is a stopping point asking for commitment and defense. Insight is a fragment awareness that invites further exploration. Intellect tends to enshrine its truth, while soul hopes that insights will keep coming until some degree of wisdom is achieved. Wisdom is the marriage of intellects longing for truth and souls acceptance of the labyrinthine nature of the human condition."

Anyone can turn to religion or spiritual practice as a way out of the twists and turns of ordinary life. We hope to transcend the confinement and routine in life, by looking beyond our lives. Hope lies in raising above ordinary life with feelings of being pure and unfettered.

.

MEDITATION

We can experience the realm beyond without having a Near-death Experience. We can access the realm beyond through meditation. Meditation provides an easy method to rise beyond the body naturally and comfortably. People can make this connection with the inner Light. We don't have to pass from this physical life into death, to accomplish this.

"Mystics and saints of various religions provide us with numerous references to the inner Light. Descriptions of divine Light and of heavenly realms are given in the Bible. Christ said, "If thine eyes be single, thy whole body shall be full of Light." (Matthew 6:22)

In speaking of the inner light and sound, Saint Rajinder Singh, great saint and master of meditation says, "The aspirant sees the real Light within him, where normally the inner eye is covered by a thick veil of darkness. He then realizes that the tradition of the lighted candle found in churches and temples is to remind him of the divine Light of Heaven within.

This Light grows to the radiance of several suns put together as he advances on the way. He understands that the unceasing internal Sound he contacts within is the Divine Link called, 'word', by Christ, 'Kalma and Nida-I-Asmani' in the Koran, 'nad' in the Vedas, 'Udgit' in the Upanishads, 'sraosha' by the Zorastrians, and 'Naam' and 'Shahd' by the saints and masters."

In the 15th century, in India, meditation was taught as a science by such great saints as Guru Nanak and Kabir Sahib. Meditation can be taught as a science to anyone, irrespective of religious backgrounds. The purpose is so people can rise above their bodies to seek the spiritual realms to experience the peace, joy and bliss for themselves.

This meditation experience is described in the same ways as those describing Near-death Experiences. Both involve the entering into a world of pure Light. In Near-death Experiences, people are just entering into the threshold of the spirit world, they are then returned to their physical bodies. People who meditate cross the threshold of the spirit realm to explore inner regions. In Near-death Experiences, as in meditation can explore further to find brighter light and more ethereal realms.

Kabair and Saomi Ji Maharaji have explored inner realms, describing varying bright Lights. They also describe hearing an "inner celestial music." There are different planes created by the flow of Light and music from God. "There is a supracausal plane that contains a predominance of spirit and a thin veil of illusion. Then there is a region in which there are equal parts spirit and matter known as the causal plane. The astral plane contains more matter and less of spirit. Thus, the density of matter increased as the current flowed farther from God."

Mainstream religion teaches us that when the physical body dies, the soul departs. We know that the soul is not made up of matter, but is an ethereal substance, unlike the physical body. A person returning from an NDE, describes having a body of Light. In this physical plane, we cannot see these bodies of Light. They are beyond our ability to see, being on a plane of different vibrational rate and into a realm closer to what we know as the infrared range.

"The mechanics of the meditation process is that of connecting the soul within us with the current of Light and Sound as a method of traveling out of the physical body. When this connection occurs, we can then merge and travel with it to the higher, spiritual realms."

We identify ourselves so fully by our body and our mind, we have forgotten the essence of who we are. We focus on the physical appearance most of all, that defines who we are. Even our mind, our intelligence has become secondary to the importance of what we look like. Yet the soul, the essence and energy of who we are, is the same essence as God. God of All, is love, joy and peace. We need to seek these things which are our true nature that fill us with bliss. By identifying ourselves with our soul, we can experience divine Light and the love within ourselves.

We need also to recognize our immortality, and the death of our physical bodies will no longer hold the fear that death has always held for us. The soul does not die, it lives on as can be experienced through Meditation.

Our soul cannot enter into the spiritual realms until it is freed of all negative thought. Meditation requires full concentrated focus, without negative interference. With the knowledge we gain of what lies beyond this physical life, we can give comfort and strength to those around us.

A Meditation Technique to Discover the Spiritual Self

Meditation is a technique by which deep stillness and attention is focused to the very source of thought. By tuning out the outer world, we tune into the depth of our inner self to access a higher consciousness. It is a discipline of the mind and body as a means to strengthen our self-awareness and spirituality.

Meditation is a powerful tool for spiritual and personal growth, opening our minds to a greater understanding of life and our relationship to life.

We understand life by our experiences. Being human, our predisposed religious beliefs and society and its attitudes regarding death, block our awareness and our true comprehension of death and beyond. To most all of humanity, death remains a great mystery. We may only know the absolute truth when we experience it ourselves. Meanwhile, we can imagine, read information being published and theorize what the experience will be like.

We consciously leave our physical bodies every night in sleep, traveling to the astral plane, being the closest thing to death we experience now. Meditation is practiced along the same principles, during a waking state, relaxing the body and mind to experience a more focused, dreamlike state.

Meditation should be a part of a person's daily routine. Like anything else we do, the more it is practiced the more perfected we can become at Meditation. It should always be practiced in a place where there will be no outside distractions. Everything involves awareness of what you focus on.

To begin, find a comfortable place to sit, back straight and feet flat on the floor to align the chakras. This will enable you to receive higher vibrations. Be aware of your body, focus on your deep breathing, bringing in the good air, exhaling the old, stale air in the lungs. Envision your body filling with earth energies, feeling centered and grounded.

Visualize a powerful white light coming down into your head, surrounding and energizing. It penetrates and re-energizes throughout your body. Clear your mind of outside thought and feelings removing the energy of others from you. Imagine a vacuum cleaner, suctioning away the negative, burdensome thoughts and feelings until you feel lighter, happier and freer. Now envision a pure white, protective light surrounding you. Your mind should be receptive and aware.

To find the light of life within you, visualize a garden filled with the beauty of the flowers of your choosing. Take in the beauty surrounding you. In the garden also stands a mirror. Walk to the mirror and look at the image reflected back to you. See your face and body as they are now in as much detail as you can.

Staring at yourself in the mirror, focus on the expectations others have of you. See the areas that need forgiveness and situations for which you feel guilty. Bring love into the image with the people and situations. Envision the light of love emanating from your heart touching everyone and everything. Let that light of love touch and surround you also.

Step away from the mirror and envision once again, the garden with its large, brightly colored flowers, green grass, blue sky and warm sunlight. Your awareness is of the loving spiritual entity you are.

This is one example of a very simple Meditation that can aid in improving the way that a person feels about themselves. The more a person can practice Meditational skills that are flooded with positive love and forgiveness, the better the outside world looks and the happier that person becomes. It is not only the Meditation but the influence of positive energy that strengthens us to endure any hardship. Meditation and understanding are two very important aspects of the healing process after suffering loss.

Energy: Our Essence

Our thoughts, our attitudes and our emotions are all forms of energy, constantly influencing the world around us. Physicists no long consider themselves detached observers. They know their very presence influences the properties of the particle/waves they study. Our attitudes affect the cycles within and around us. Aware of this, the Tao people live consciously, respectfully, knowing they exert a powerful influence on their world. Most people are unaware of this even though it has been proven scientifically.

Not only do we influence people around us; we are continually affected by the actions and attitudes of others. Spending time with other people means breathing the same air, sharing the same energy field. Some interaction is energizing. Others deplete us, draining our energy which we can feel, clearly and distinctly. Being exhausted after being together with someone, the person is draining your energy. Unbalanced, uncentered, out of touch with the source of "chi" in their lives, such people subsist on energy transfusions from others. These people are emotional vampires.

Emotional vampires are always clamoring for help. Whenever something goes wrong, they run to a strong friend to rescue them, acting so helpless that others feel guilty refusing to listen. Attaching themselves like barnacles, these people become increasingly demanding and dependent. They do not have the abilities to deal with problems in their lives, so this dumping process is a habit in which they circumvent taking responsibility for themselves.

This is important knowledge for those trying to cope with significant loss of a spouse of loved one. Those are the people who are most vulnerable and need to feel needed. They need reinforcement to their own self-worth. People who have low self-esteem often get caught up in the negative energies of others. Their insecurity and confusion makes them vulnerable to manipulators and emotional vampires.

We can transcend hostile cycles in our personal lives - in relationships, health, careers, and finances. We can also overcome hostile cycles in society. Whether these cycles are great or small, personal or universal, the way to transcend them is by centering, nonresistance and taking positive action. When a person can keep themselves centered and in balance, they have the ability to endure whatever comes to them.

Succumbing to fear or guilt only empowers manipulators who draw us into negativity. We give what inevitably comes back to us. Negativity begets negativity. Nonresistance neutralizes negative cycles. When our heart and minds are no longer troubled by negative emotions, we can act wisely, defusing negativity with wisdom of the Tao. Nonresistance helps us shift from negative to positive. When no one overreacts, the hostile cycle winds down.

Resisting change leads to depression, emotional drain and exhaustion. Positive action rebuilds self-esteem. Maintaining a standard of order is positive action, breaking the negative cycle. The first law of the universe is order, and we need to respect the natural order within and around us.

Sometimes the action we take to heal our lives also brings healing to others. When working through the process of grieving, the time will come when the confusion subsides and a person will feel a need to help others. By applying the knowledge gained through the experience of loss, we can bring others to the understanding we have achieved. Reaching out to help also takes us along the path to complete healing and gives us insights into new opportunities.

Our physical bodies do not become strong unless we put the necessary nutrients into them. Our spiritual-self does not progress without proper care either. We grow as we increase in knowledge. Some growth is easy and painless, but some comes only after trial and tears. The easy, painless changes, as in our behavior, are surface changes. Major changes are a result of harsh, life-changing events. These are the essential, deep, spiritual changes, with deeper meaning and purpose.

LIFE CYCLES

We live in a world of ups and downs, of negative and positive, of prosperity and hardship. As the physical seasons change, so do the life cycles change. A summer gives us feelings of hope, joy, warmth, growth and prosperity, alas, the winters are perceived as dormancy, where there is little growth, little prosperity within ourselves. The cycles of life are comparative to the cycles in nature. But the low cycles need not remain or be accepted as a change in the cyclic pattern, only as a temporary lull in our lives that give us time to seek awareness and assimilate that which can raise the cycle into balance and harmony.

Understanding this principle can give a person inner knowledge and strength to work through the low cycles and begin moving forward. As the seasons of nature, there is a time to be born and a time to die. The seasons of birth bring us great joy at the existence of new life. The seasons of death, approached with understanding can also bring us a season of joy, as death is not the ending but the beginning of life on a different plane, without the pains and anchors that come with a physical body. The body having served its purpose, has broken down to return from whence it came. But the essence of the whole person, the soul or spirit lives on, in a place where a physical body is no longer needed.

Any loss is in essence, a positive transition, as the old dying away so the new can present itself to us. For every time, there is a purpose and to shed what once was, opens doors to opportunity for the new. Crisis brings change, that people have great difficulty accepting. We like consistency, structure and routine in our lives. When change, as in death comes our way, it can bring us to the path of new horizons, new awareness and understanding. It prepares us for what lies ahead, though at the time the reasons are unclear and life seems only harsh and cruel. Our choices, our decisions in our lives take us to our intended destiny.

As a society, overall, we have evolved into self-centeredness and materialism, turning away because of the nature of who we are, from the spiritual beings we truly are. Crises, redirects us, gives us the opportunity to evaluate who we are, where we have been and to evolve back into beings of self-awareness and redevelop awareness to those around us and the needs that are present. I cannot accept that we were given life on this earth to ignore other life forms around us. If that was the case, we would hardly have evolved past the isolated lives of Adam and Eve. We were intended to love and be loved, to share, caring for our fellow man.

When a major disaster strikes a city or county, people spontaneously reach out to help those around them, making certain their physical and emotional needs are met. But why, does this only happen when disaster steps in, causing chaos and hardship and death? The true nature of who we are, overrides the creatures we have come to be, and we find a deep sense of love and concern for our fellow man that on a normal basis is buried so deep within us, we hardly regard its existence.

The loss of things to natural disasters teaches that material possessions can be lost as easily as they were gained and their value has nothing to do with the value of life or who we are. Loss of parts of our bodies, due to accident or illness teaches us we can still function as the wholeness is within the spirit of who we are. The loss of a loved one gives us understanding of how fragile life is and each moment is a treasure. The person whom we have lost has contributed greatly to who we are and though they are physically no longer present, the essence of who they were and what they gave us in life, lives forever in the memories we have of them. Our lives are intended to go on, for a purpose. Be it to finish a job yet undone or to help someone else through the life's journey they have embarked upon, having the same influence on them, as the influence of our lost love was over us. We have faced death and can positively help those around us face death without fear. We can help them understand it is a natural part of the life cycle.

Our grief, is for ourselves and the losses we have sustained. We are given the opportunity for growth and greater fulfillment by reaching out and bringing others to the profound knowledge we have gained, because of our own experience. Whatever we choose to do with that knowledge is up to us, but the cycles of life and death continue to go on, all around us. When suffering a life-changing loss, you will find it is the time when you need most desperately for someone, for anyone, to understand what is happening, someone to listen with empathy and help guide you through the steps of recovery toward a full and normal life once again.

DREAMS

The dream, far from being the confusion of haphazard and meaningless associations it is commonly believed to be, or a result merely of somatic sensations during sleep, is autonomous and meaningful product of psychic activity, susceptible, like all other psychic functions, of a systematic analysis.

Dreams, like every complex product, are creations, pieces of work that have motives, they are trains of antecedent associations. Dreaming has meaning and purpose, like everything else we do. Freud felt that the common experience, be it psychic or physical, is not accidental. Events which do not stimulate strong emotions, have little, if any, influence on our thoughts or actions. Those that provoke strong reactions play a tremendous role in our psychological development.

In dreams, we encounter emotional components for it is easy to understand that all the products of psychic activity depend on the strongest influences. Our lives are spent struggling for the realization of our desires. It is for this that we work and why we think. Religious and philosophical systems of people in every age are proof of this. The thought of immortality, even in a philosophical guise, is no other than a wish, for which philosophy is but the facade.

Freud says, "Every dream represents the fulfillment of a repressed wish." Freud also tells us, "The wishes which form the dream thought are never desires which one openly admits to oneself, but desires that are repressed because of their painful character; and it is because they are excluded from conscious reflection in the waking state that they float up, indirectly, in dreams."

Dreams have a psychic structure unlike that of other contents of consciousness. They show no continuity of development that are so typical of conscious content. Dreams do not arise like other conscious content from discernable, logical and emotional continuity, but rather are the remnants of a peculiar psychic activity taking place during sleep.

Dreams can baffle, many times, attempts at recollection even immediately after waking. Some can be remembered with doubtful accuracy yet few can be recalled with clarity and distinction. Often after the loss of a loved one, a person will dream of seeing or actually being with the deceased. These dreams remain clear and vivid, they do not fade with the passing of time. There is almost always a clear message given with the vision of the loved one. It is almost always one of comfort, letting the dreamer know that they have gone on to a far better place, that they are happy where they are. So are these dreams or are they taking place in new reality on another plane of existence?

Those who study dreams and the dreamers, see a distinct difference between normal dreaming and those who have survived the loss of a loved one and dream of them returning to give comfort and reassurance. The latter are clearly different and meaningful at a time when this type of consolation are needed. The dreams remain crystal clear in memory, not fading with time. The interpretation is clear, it is a message intended to give us peace. It has also been shown that these dreams are a significant aid in the healing after a loss.

The ancients looked to their dreams and their dead for guidance and prophecy. The Koran states that dreams that bring us good news, are the truest of them all. Dreams have given us new theories, beautiful sonatas, time-saving machines and changes of the ways in which a person views the world. "Dreams, for centuries have brought inspiration for scientists, artists,, musicians, inventors and mourners alike," says Dr. LeGrand.

"Dreams are one of the most frequent modes of communication between survivors and their deceased loved ones. Many religions are replete with history and decision-making based on information received in dreams." The experience is most beneficial to those mourning the loss of a loved one.

How can dreams help us, while grieving the loss of a loved one? Once a person understands that the experience was more like a living dream, being a realistic part of loss, experienced for the purpose of giving us comfort, peace and understanding that life goes on after physical death, and love survives the grave, the easier we come to accept death itself. If the dreams are repetitive in nature, then there is more of a message that the survivor has not understood. There is unfinished business that needs looking into, or an unresolved issue we need to confront. The concerns have passed on, with the loved one and he/she will not rest until there is resolution. This also is true, when someone has been prematurely taken from life, as in murder or suicide, and needs to express information for resolution.

The Origin of Dreams

Are dreams of the deceased truly the deceased or the dreamers mind? One very significant concept in dream interpretation is that our dreams are honest, trustworthy representations of our inner life at any given time. The unconscious, from which dreams originate, are for the benefit of the dreamer. Jung suggested that dreams are a product of the unconscious mind.

"It is the realm of the spirit, the place of healing energy, the abode of God's spirit within us," says Dr. Clyde H. Reid. Without a doubt, dreams can be a spiritual source.

Dreams of the death of someone we know may not necessarily have predictive qualities. They usually are stimulated by psychological causes such as negative feelings the dreamer has toward the person, or withdrawal from a relationship have been suggested. When the dream of someone dying does come true shortly after the dream, it is usually, according to authorities, to conscious awareness of illness or eminent death, though they are not fully aware of it.

We each must decide, if dreaming of the death of a loved one, whether the dreams are metaphors or telepathic communication the brain receives from outside of ourselves. Some are actual predictive dreams, regarding the death of a loved one. It has been suggested by Dr. Le Grand that these predictive dreams may come from, "a whole side of us that operates outside of space and time." He considers a region of our brain that communicates with the mystical, calling it the 'God Sensor', functioning like a sixth sense.

A dream that may have significance beyond the usual will stand out clearly and distinctly from all the rest. We normally forget our dreams easily, sometimes immediately. Dreams of the deceased and predictive dreams stand out above the rest. You remember them in great detail, the message clear. Dreams of visitation by the deceased can create a completeness within us, bringing us to the point of closure. These dreams allow us joyful, pleasant memories of the deceased rather than recollections that bring us pain of loss.

Dreams, Open Doors to Insight

According to Cayce, "Each night the soul compares in dreams - as it does in prayerful or inspired reflection - the behavior of the person with the dearest and richest universal patterns that the soul has grasped and chosen. To be sure, dreams and visions might emerge from and reflect or advance many levels of the psyche at work. But the overall action of the soul in sleep or waking is ever for richness and integration, as it journeys toward wholeness and productive love with God." During times of crisis, we need to be able to study the self and self-experiences.

Our dreams can bring us needed insights to lead us through crises to inventiveness and growth. Under laboratory conditions, is has been shown that the psyche judiciously tracks and symbolizes the progress of growth episodes themselves. They show dreams advancing the action not just mirroring it. In dreams we move life energies through appointed rounds to new growth. It is necessary to work with dream content to re-balance the psyche and rework its dynamics until there is correlation with daytime activity and relationships that enhance the competence we need.

Recalling dreams can take practice until it becomes a skill. All can recall dreams, even those amid crisis, if they choose to do so. It is necessary to want to know the inner world and have someone to share dreams with on a fairly regular basis. It helps to keep a running log of dreams, writing them down after awakening. The last dream of the night is usually the longest and the easiest to recall upon waking. We also have the ability to train ourselves to waken after each dream sequence, and write them down. This, however, does take work and training. When in a crisis situation, it would be best, to focus more on the dream most clear in the mind, upon awakening.

"The unconscious goes on reworking and regrouping our experiences and relationships all our lives, toward deeper insight and growth, it does not give up recall if its dream treasures to those who say to it, 'Yes, but'," says Cayce. When writing down dreams, to include feelings, what took place and where, the writer usually will have a sense of little bits of meaning. Underlining words and phrases that are clear and distinct can aid in separating the incidental from the central parts of dream content.

Correlating ones dreams with the waking life, helps in the study and interpretation of dreams. Listing what takes place in the large areas of our daily lives (love and relationships, work and study, growth, faith, selfhood in physical, mental and spiritual levels) help us sort our dreams and match them to our concerns.

Being equipped with vast comparative resources, and since it is we ourselves who create our dream structure for reasons that a part of us already knows, there should be no difficulty in interpreting those dreams. If a dream, as a message, is wrongly handled, we can be sure in knowing it will repeat itself. Sensitive responses to our dreams are far more important than a structured decoding of the symbolism. Sharing them, writing them, drawing them, listening to them and trying a new course of action because of their message, self-study and self-training, open doors of opportunity to receive the gifts our dreams offer to us. Our dreams can give us the answers we seek, if we listen to what they tell us.

Carl Jung's' view, as well as Edgar Cayce's' view of growth or karma, are that the resources of all recurrent human experience are in principle, available to us. Dismay and pain in crises open to us our inner selves and show us a path to depths we never knew existed. Nature may remind us that growth has its seasons.

Dreams and Crises of the Heart

When losing someone dear to us, someone we truly love, we lose a part of ourselves as well. This kind of loss permanently changes us. Love is the strongest bond we have, transcending death. When consciousness alters, as in states of sleep, meditation, prayer, in visions or in pain, then it may align itself, momentarily, with the reality of after-death existence to allow love to touch the beloved.

Much discussion on visitation from deceased loved ones indicate that over half of widows and widowers have had contact with the dearly departed, visually. Greater yet are parents who have lost a child to death, who have had visions of the deceased child, within one year after the child has passed on. Ideally, dreams are the means by which this contact has been made and the message is the same; the dead are alive, well and happy on the other side, and love does not die. The dreams give comfort to those left behind, as intended.

There are several distinguishing features of such dreams. The beloved may appear as a memory, or as a symbol of their own unique qualities. Some may step through a doorway surrounded by soft light as we see them on the next plane of existence. They look to us, as they did at their peak age -

whole and vital. It is not a frightening scene, there are rarely tears and resulting feelings are joyful and hopeful of being together once again, on the other side.

Dreams suggest our loved ones watch over us, encourage us or warn us of impending danger which also leads us to believe they are near to protect us. Cayce's view, supported in such dreams, is that, "the soul that has traveled through death, moves increasingly into new orbits of awareness and growth, from which it may dip back into our lives, yet still keep its forward motion."

From my own experience, my crisis lead me to feeling like a failure. I was losing my home, had lost my job, and was heading into bankruptcy court. It was the lowest point of my life and I was filled with despair. The night before I was to go into court, I had a dream that remains clear to me to this day. My husband came to me, in a fashion that I would recognize him. He held me in his arms and told me I was not a failure that everything would be okay. At the time, I thought it was just a dream. But I knew that if he were there, he would have done that very thing to give me comfort.

Since that time, and after much intense and deep study, I firmly believe my husband returned to let me know, everything would be okay and he did not see me as a failure at all. His presence gave me peace and understanding that all I could do was go forward with what I had available to me. At that time, I had very little to go with, but it was sufficient to get me through. I had not been visited before that time nor have I been visited since. But it was a time I truly needed that kind of reassurance from the man I had so deeply loved.

Dreams of the Deceased

"Dreams are a mystery. Dreams are a source of wisdom and self-knowledge. Dreams are a normal and healthy part of grieving," says Dr. LeGrand.

These statements are accurate and yet fail to include the fact that dreams bring relief to survivors, when life feels so empty and meaningless after losing a loved one to death. Our dreams take us into realms of other realities. From these realities we can gain insights to understanding self, accessing knowledge to benefit all of humanity. Dreams occur nightly to everyone though they may not all seem important. Yet dreams can do many things, including having the capacity to bring us joy and peace of mind.

Dreaming of the deceased contribute greatly to giving us comfort and support in times of duress. Dreams have brought survivors reassurance that they can make it through whatever life deals them. A single dream can make all the difference in the way the survivor feels and approaches the problems ahead of them.

It needs to be known, that dreams can bring sadness as well if not perceived as they are given to us. Once the dreamer understands the purpose of dreaming of the deceased is to let him or her know they are fine and happy on the other side, the dreams don't taunt us, but give a positive message of the continuation of life, on a different plane.

Dreams can give us guidance and advice for making positive adjustments in areas of our lives. They can bring us to the realization we need to change direction, bringing us back into balance. Dreams can also be a means by which we can say good-bye or say what we felt was left unsaid at the time of death. They can help us to release the chains that firmly hold us to the past and aid in the process of letting go of something no longer ours to hold.

There are no blanket interpretations to dreams. A person must evaluate what has taken place in the dream for the message there and what it means. It should be interpreted according to the dreamers current waking behavior and thinking. Several possibilities may come to mind, the one that feels right is what should be considered correct. What the dream means to the dreamer should take precedence over what someone else interprets the dream to mean.

.

CHANGE

Since this is an on-going situation we will all be involved in, at some time in our lives, by using our crises and the knowledge we have gained, to become agents to change the approach humanity takes toward death and aggressively bring people to a greater awareness of what takes place and how we can prepare ourselves for it. Change can only come from experiencing the hardships of crisis when losing someone we love. The actual loss, is only the beginning of a long, hard journey into transition.

The solutions we find must empower us as the survivors as well as those we work with. We must have the ability to empathize, yet remain strong, honest and practical with information that is liberating. It must be understood that in crisis, wishes are not always fulfilled. Loss contains a higher purpose that only becomes clear with hindsight.

The focus should be on the immediate situation, the current needs that require attention. When working with the dying, the importance is presence, listening and meeting the immediate needs. In working with the survivors, the focus is understanding death, loss and the process of grief, each step being an essential one into healing.

Death is not God, as we tend to equate the two. Any more than the magic trick is the magician. Like birth or illness or old age, death is just another event along the way.

Kabir says, "If you don't break your ropes while you're alive, do you think ghosts will do it after? The idea that the soul will join with the ecstatic just because the body is rotten, that is all fantasy. What is found now is found then. If you find nothing now, you will simply end up with an empty apartment in the City of Death. If you make love with the divine now, in the next life you will have the face of satisfied desire."

Do not be looking elsewhere for your true nature. Do not think of it as something coming, but instead recognize it as the ever present possibility in each moment.

Doorways to Awareness

The pains that a person suffers, the loneliness one feels, experiences that disappointed us, addictions and pitfalls in life are doorways to awareness. Each offers an opportunity to see beyond the illusion that serves in the balancing and growth of one's soul.

Within each experience of pain or negativity lies the opportunity to challenge the perception behind it, the fear that is there within it, and to choose to learn with wisdom.

Clarity is the perception of wisdom. It is seeing with wisdom and learning to choose to learn through wisdom, rather than fear and doubt. Clarity allows a person to experience their fellow humans with compassion rather than judgment. It allows the energy of the heart to flow freely.

As I have walked the path to awareness, I have found within myself a sensitivity to the emotional energies of those around me. Daily I encounter those who are floundering with a sense of grief, having lost someone to divorce, having lost a career, a home, a child, a way of life.

Rather than acknowledging there are those who understand and can help them come to an understanding of what is taking place, their thoughts turn to hopelessness and despair. They see no opportunity before them as they have no understanding of transition. Understanding brings knowledge and from knowledge comes hope, from which possibility becomes visible.

There are steps that need to be taken, that raise people to the different levels of comfort and awareness. Each level brings us to the ultimate goal of healing. By approaching the event of death and loss in an open manner, we can have the ability to learn that these are transitions, necessary in life, to help us to return to a path from which we have strayed. These transitions have purpose, and there are times when the lessons we have in life are meant to shake us to a point of hitting bottom, so we must look at who we are and start over. Through the pain, we must have the ability to see the door of opportunity that stands open, awaiting us to just step through it.

Organized Religion Today

Organized religion today is based on fear. In time of dire need, how can we fall back on religion that tells us we are sinners and destined for eternal damnation unless we meet certain criteria? So many cannot, and this is the onset of the search for their true spirituality.

As a child I was raised in a strict, Evangelical Christian environment. My recollection of church attendance does not bring about fond memories of any kind, in fact quite the opposite is true. A small child has no interest in church doctrine, or politics, and I was too young to understand, so boredom set in easily. Church attendance was a ritual and mandatory, though I came to dread Sunday's arrival, every week.

My memories clearly hold visions of hellfire and brimstone. To me, while very young, it was like a thrilling ghost tale. As I grew older, to a better understanding, I was shocked to learn that this was what the future held for those who did not accept Jesus into their hearts, and were always doing good. I was a mischievous child, so to my way of understanding, hell was my destiny.

I realized I could never achieve the perfection that was expected of me to reach a heavenly plane. The faith I was expected to maintain, was based on the fear of eternal damnation. God's laws were impossible to keep, in the eyes of a child, especially when it seemed like every time I turned around, I was in trouble. I was told I was a sinner, in the church setting and in the family unit.

I was never seen as an individual, I was part of a greater plan, one little lamb in a whole herd of sheep. Individual talents weren't encouraged, I was taught to be a follower, being told how to behave and what to believe,, according to a strict, unbending religious structure.

Like so many, the day came when I walked the long aisle to bow down before God and accept Jesus as Savior. I think I expected to be struck by lightning. The reason I had gone forward was due to the alternative I'd been hearing about. I faced the bowels of hell, if I didn't.

The strategy used is fear, leading people to believe their souls are at stake which drives them to accept whatever is necessary to achieve eternal reward. Emphasis within the church is put on the original sin and the fall.

A curse that hangs over the heads of all mankind until they 'see the light' and avoid the horrors that will most certainly befall them, if they don't.

Throughout the history of Christianity, the divine and the diabolical are intertwined; God of Light, Prince of Darkness, the paradise of the Garden of Eden and the presence of the serpent offering up temptation, heaven and hell, black and white and the narrow, bumpy path of good vs the wide, smooth avenue of sin.

When death lurks around the corner and we are looking at taking that last breath, what comes to mind isn't the knowledge of transition into another plane of existence into bliss. The thoughts are fear driven as to whether we will find ourselves eternally damned to suffer hell fires. Because of religious indoctrination in physical life, we fear the inevitability of death. We don't have to face death this way.

Death of the physical body is inevitable for all living things. As a society we are of the opinion that if we ignore something, it doesn't exist or won't happen to us. That is our general, overall, approach to the subject of death. It isn't until death or loss impacts our personal arena of existence, that we begin to look at it and understand something about it.

We focus on our lives in the ways of success or failure, physical appearance, money, property, assets, offspring, anything of a physical nature that can be seen by people at large. That is our societal view of who we are. Our lives are based around what we have, not who we are nor what we have to contribute to this life less than monetary in value.

Events that occur in our lives that cause material loss are not accepted as a form of death, they are perceived as failures. Not only by ourselves, but by others. If we perceived them as loss and mini-steps to educate us for the inevitable physical death, we would find ourselves more accepting of the reality of death. When climbing a ladder, one must put one foot above te other to step up to another rung, to progress upward.

This means letting go of the old rung to rise to a new one. The same is true in life. Each step is a lesson that leads us to greater knowledge but we must leave the old ways behind us to progress. By ignoring the lessons we are given, we refuse the knowledge to be gained. In everything, even tragedy, we can find a positive lesson and outcome. We only need to open our hearts and our minds to the possibilities.

Organized religion is focused on the living. It is not designed for the dead. It prepares us to fear the day we meet death, not accept it as a natural process in the cycle of life and enfold and endear it as a transition. In learning about death, we can come to a far better understanding of life.

We need to learn about unconditional love, letting go of the negative emotions of guilt, hate, anger, bias, jealousy, resentment and blinding fear. Negative emotion can burden and anchor us not only in physical life, but in death as well.

Once we learn to love without condition, forgive and let go of old negative patterns, we find our lives are filled with richness never experienced before. We find an inner peace we have been seeking and harmony in all we do. This is bliss, which we all seek.

We come to learn about the soul, the energy of who we are, that transcends physical death. To do so we need to let go of the confines of structured religious beliefs that we are indoctrinated into that limit our thinking and close our minds to the reality that we are spiritual beings, part of a Universal Consciousness.

To learn that understanding ourselves is to understand the concept of God. We are each a part of what comprises a far larger picture, like each piece in a jigsaw puzzle is essential to the completed picture.

Death is an opportunity for the living to come to a far greater understanding of transition and new direction. We can learn to have a greater understanding of our emotions through understanding the soul.

We can come to the awareness of having purpose in life, whether we know the exact purpose or not, what we do influences the direction of people and circumstances around us.

Everything we do has an effect around us, whether we are hurtful or helpful, one day, beyond this physical life, we will review our every word and deed and the impact it had. We will feel the hurt of those we hurt and the joys of those we gave happiness to in life. We become our own judge and jury as we review these things from our physical lives, to forgive or to be less forgiving of ourselves is a decision we make alone.

When losing a loved one to physical death, we grieve. We feel a lifetime of emotions we have endured and potentially suppressed during our lifetime. It is a time of hardship, non-understanding and pain that goes to the core of who we are. I firmly believe as we take each step toward learning and growth in life that we come to know death in a more intimate way. The period of grief is therefore, but a small indicator of what we will find as we face our panoramic life review after death. How we deal with the tumult of emotions in grief suggests how we shall deal with the life we review after death.

If we cannot deal with the feelings of loneliness and guilt, of fear of the unknown, condemnation of others, of hate toward God for our losses, we will find we cannot forgive ourselves for these feelings on the other side of life. It is essential that we learn the value of the lessons given in life that teach us ultimately how to let go and free ourselves from anchors in death.

As a society, we have done little to research the event of death. There are those who have given a lifetime of work to the dying and what we are able to learn from them. They give great insight into the fact that the soul progresses onto another plane of existence and there is great joy to be found there. Far more work needs to be done in counseling the grieving and understanding the process of death in this physical life. We have the means and a portion of the knowledge we need, we now need to focus more attention onto the subject and begin the real education to benefit us all.

As a Metaphysician and Practitioner, this is my goal. To reach out to those who have tremendous fear and little understanding of life after life. The work I intend to continue coincides with the work of scientists, physicists and medical professionals who are expanding the research and knowledge in this field. This is something everyone will have to confront at some time in their lives as there is no escaping it. Thus lies the crux of how important this work is and will be. As a Minister of Metaphysics, I do not believe in death but I do believe death is a transition into a continuation of life. The energy, or life spirit continues on discarding the physical body, which returns to the elements. The energy of the spirit, of who we are, continues on into another plane of higher consciousness.

"By perhaps understanding our own reality we can better understand our lives in relation to our transition from it." (Rites of the Metaphysical Ministry) "Death is certain for the born. Rebirth is certain for the dead." Kahlil Gibran tell us, You would know the secret of death, but how shall you find it unless you seek it in the heart of life? The owl whose night-bound eyes are blind unto the day cannot unveil the mystery of light. If you would indeed behold the spirit of death, open your heart wide unto the body of life.

For life and death are one, even as the river and the sea are one. In the depth of your hopes and desires, less your silent knowledge of the beyond; And like seeds dreaming beneath the snow your heart dreams of spring. Trust the dreams for in them is the hidden gate to eternity. Your fear of death is but the trembling of the shepherd when he stands before the king whose hand is to be laid upon him in honor.

Is the shepherd not joyful beneath his trembling, that he shall wear the mark of the king? Yet his is more mindful of his trembling? For what is it to die but to stand naked in the wind and melt into the sun? And what is it to cease breathing, but to free the breath from its restless tides that it may rise and expand and seek God unencumbered? Only when you have reached the mountain top, then shall you begin to climb. And when the earth shall claim your limbs, then shall you truly dance."

The subject of death is like new, unexplored territory and yet it has been as much a part of us as life since the beginning of time. It is just recently that we have had the bravest explorers step out to discuss the truth in something very much feared by all. We have pioneers who work with the dying, learning from their last words as to what they feel and what they see beyond this life. Before they pass, they reveal much, if only we take the time to listen. But we fear what we do not know, and though we don't speak of it, we view death of the physical body as the ending. We couldn't be more wrong about it.

We have scientific equipment that can aid us in the quest for answers, yet few use it. It has been shown that upon the death of the physical body, there is a loss of three-quarters of a pound, which we can only speculate to be the soul, leaving the body. This is physical evidence of the life spirit going on, that a part of us does go on, into another realm of existence.

Few are accepting of this scientific information because if we wish not to believe something, we will make any excuse not to. So much more needs to be done in this field of research as we are just barely breaking ground in this area. Those having Near Death Experiences are finally able to come forward with what they have seen, heard and felt having left the physical body. They return with stories of awe and pure bliss in what they have found on the other side of this physical life. Yet most of these stories are attributed to chemical changes in the brain, the lack of oxygen and are not accepted for the value they hold.

Our religious barriers go up, as we are told to expect to find heaven or hell. This, in the research work I have been doing and in the work of many others, does not appear to be the case at all. Yet we are taught to believe and accept this because of the doctrine of our churches. We have come a long way in so many areas, to expand upon and improve our life styles. Yet when it comes to the mysteries in life, we remain ignorant and unaccepting. It is easier to remain within the confines of our comfort levels and not question that which we do not know. It isn't until death or loss hit us in the face, and we experience the constituents of that loss, that we touch the depth of our souls, to seek the answers of the experience. Unfortunately, it takes a tragedy for us to come unto the truth of our spiritual selves.

QUANTUM PHYSICS AND
THE LANGUAGE OF PRAYER

We are teaching a motif that allows a person to break out of a rut that they no longer wish to remain within. Many people find themselves on a road that they we no longer want to travel, so what can they do about it? This article presents some lost knowledge that has been recorded in the Dead Sea Scrolls that enables us to make those life changes we need to make now. By making the changes we will not be trapped with regrets, fears or excess baggage upon our death and discover we still have to work out those issues or else remain anchored to this physical plane.

Not everything we do is about the investigations of ghosts. We also teach how not to be anchored to the earth plane.

The Language of Prayer has not evolved from the Christian era, but five hundred years before the birth of Jesus. It was practiced at a remote desert Essene community of Qumran, along the Dead Sea whose residents lived close to nature. The Essene Masters taught many principles that were later adopted by Christianity, but they originated from the ancient Hebrew Bible used by the Essenes called the Dead Sea Scrolls.

These scrolls were hidden in caves above the Dead Sea and discovered in 1947. The caves held many scrolls that contained fragmented text from the Hebrew Bible. This desert community practiced a spiritual way of life. Its members were called the Sons of Light. They lived according to the teachings of their Hebrew Bible. The knowledge and understanding found in the Dead Sea Scrolls became corrupted by the fourth century A.D. so the Essene Masters sent copies of the scrolls to the four corners of earth to preserve the original text.. Teachings from the Essene scrolls have been found in Tibet and in the American Southwest among some Native American tribes.

The Dead Sea Scrolls are important as they are the oldest text of the Hebrew Bible which predates the preChristian era by five hundred years. Their language has not changed in two thousand years so the text language is still the Hebrew that is the language of the people. The Dead Sea Scrolls have not been translated and re-translated as have the many versions of the Bible that we currently use today.

In order to understand the full impact of the Language of Prayers, we must first understand some basic Quantum physics principles that have been validated today under laboratory conditions. These Quantum principles validate the information that is presented in the Dead Sea Scrolls. Today's technology helps us to understand the spiritual meaning found in the Dead Sea Scrolls. I found Gregg Braden's book, Isaiah Effect very interesting. I would like to share some of his findings in this article.

Quantum theory suggests we will find the existence of many outcomes for a given moment in time. Rather than creating our reality, it may be more accurate to say that we create the conditions into which we attract future outcomes, already established, into the focus of the present.

The choices that we make as individuals determine which quantum possibility, we experience in our personal lives. Quantum Physics suggests that by redirecting our focus – where we place our attention – we bring a new course of events into focus while at the same time releasing an existing course of events that no longer serve us.

The membrane between future possibilities, may be so thin that we fail to recognize it when we cross into a new outcome. We may feel that the choice has been spontaneous or natural, the change now allows us to experience a possibility that was only a dream in the past.

Prayer is the language that allows us to express our dreams, making them real in our lives. The existence of many outcomes for a given event has been predicted by Quantum Physics for nearly eighty years.

For multiple outcomes to be considered implies that each possibility is already created and presents in our world. Perhaps in a form that we have yet to recognize, somewhere in creativity, as an embryonic mix of the physical and nonphysical, each outcome awaits to be called into the focus of our awareness. As our outcome gives way to another, for a brief moment the two must occupy the same space at the same time. As one event is brought into the focus of our senses, it must be capable of overlapping a second event, if only for the fraction of a second that it takes the two to slide past one another.

Today, Quantum Physics has validated this concept in the Bose-Einstein Condensate. This was named for the two men who predicted such an occurrence. What this means is that reality can occur during the time that two atoms occupy the same point, in the same space, at the same time. This concept has been observed and documented under laboratory conditions.

Now to the Dead Sea Scrolls . . . The Essene text suggests that the effect of prayer comes from something OTHER than the words of the prayers themselves. The secret of prayer lies beyond the words of praise, the incantations, and the rhythmic chants to the "powers that be." The Essenes invite us to LIVE the intent of our prayer in our lives. The power of prayer is found in a force that cannot be spoken or transmitted as the written word – the FEELING that the prayer's words evoke with us.

It is the FEELING of our prayers that open the door and illuminates our paths to the forces of the seen and unseen. To change the condition of our outer world, we must actually become the condition of our desire from within. The Essene elders taught that we have three conditions to have a power prayer. We must merge our thoughts and our emotions as one to create the feelings we need to become the silent language of creation.

A simple equation would be: **Feeling=Thoughts x Emotions.** We must have the product of our thoughts and our emotions to create the feeling that is necessary to obtain a new outcome.

Simply speaking prayer words have no power or effect. This is why so many prayers fail to materialize. Often we offer up negative prayers, such as "please spare my son's life" or "please heal the cancer in my daughter's body." These are prayers that focus our attention on what we do not want. We envision our son laying in a hospital bed struggling for life or we see the tumor eating the good cells in our daughter's body when we pray. These are doomed to fail. Our vision is concentrated on the death of our loved one and we want divine intervention to prevent it, but this is a negative prayer.

We need to focus on a higher choice that we chose to bring into our lives, and live from that prospective. For example, instead of praying for sparing the life of the son, visualize him running in the field, climbing trees, playing baseball, laughing, joking and having fun. This creates a different outcome, a feeling of life that you accept as reality.

You must feel his aliveness, see him running and climbing and having fun as a boy ought to have.

You focus on life, not on death and thus your prayers now take on power and life. You now envision life and health for the son, not laying ill in a hospital bed. The language of prayer is the key to life itself. It does not matter to what God you pray, but the important part is that you pray with intense feelings, your thoughts and emotions are merged as one in the feeling.

Now, I suspect we have some folks who are getting very hot under the collar now because I said that when we combine our thoughts and emotions into a strong feelings, we can pray with power.

I know that some will get excited because I did not say Jesus was the power. Did I not say that the Language of Prayer was five hundred years BEFORE the birth of Jesus? The Language of Prayer did not originate with Jesus, but He did use the Essene practice in His teachings.

Many scholars suggest Jesus learned from the Essene community at Qumran while a member of that community. Many of the His teachings were not new, but dated back to over five hundred years before. The Essenes taught about praying with all of your heart, might, mind and soul.

The power is not in the words, but in the feelings. It is being able to change the outcome to another outcome that is more acceptable. There are no good or bad outcomes, only outcomes. Do not judge them, accept them and learn from the lessons therein.

This is a very brief overview of the Language of Prayer, but there is sufficient information to enable a person to change their outcome. The Language of Prayer does not demand organized religion, but it does require us to pray with feelings. Is it any wonder that many discover that their prayers have failed to be answered? Those caught up in a problem turn to prayer for help or relief, but find their words fall on deaf ears. The faithful start to doubt their faith as their prayers go unanswered.

The Language of Prayer became corrupted, valuable portions were destroyed or changed rendering the prayer process incomplete. Most of the ancient preChristian Hebrew texts were destroyed during the Nicean Council in 325 A.D. when the council voted on the books that supported their position and the current teachings into the current 66 books of the Modern Bible.

The down side to this Council was that the many earlier Christian sects had their texts banned and destroyed because the Council wanted to unify Christianity that was acceptable to both Church and State. The Church and State wanted no competition from the other Christian or preChristian groups.

Today, many people reject these early Christian and preChristian texts as unacceptable because they were not included with the original 66 books for the modern day Bible. Many valuable texts were banned or believed destroyed by pious Church scholars who wanted to present the current trend acceptable to the Church and State.

Our spiritual path is not determined by what a Church declares to be truth, but what truth we find within ourselves. Four walls do not make truth, but becoming attuned with our inner selves does open the doors to understanding, at least according to Dr. Dave.

Some good books on the subject are: Magic Dimensions by Dr. Dave Oester and Dr. Sharon Gill, Isaiah Effect: Decoding the Lost Science of Prayer and Prophecy by Gregg Braden and Words of Light: Spiritual Wisdom from the Dead Sea Scrolls by Kenneth Hanson, Ph.D.

BIBLIOGRAPHY

Ericsson, Stephanie 1993
COMPANION THROUGH THE DARKNESS:
Inner Dialogues On Grief
New York: Harper-Collins

Bro, Harmon Hartzell, PhD. and June Avis Bro,
D.Min. 1988
GROWING THROUGH PERSONAL CRISIS
San Francisco, California: Harper and Row

Browne-Miller, Angela. 1996
EMBRACING DEATH: Riding Life's Transitions
Into Power and Freedom.
Santa Fe, New Mexico: Bear & Co.,Inc.

Jung, C.G. translated by R.F.C.Hull. 1974
DREAMS
New York: MJF Books

Kubler-Ross, Elisabeth, M.D. 1997

LIVING WITH DEATH AND DYING
New York: Simon and Schuster,Inc.

Kubler-Ross, Elisabeth, M.D. 1991
ON LIFE AFTER DEATH
Berkeley, California: Celestial Arts.

LeGrand, Louis E.,PhD. 1998
AFTER DEATH COMMUNICATIONS: Final
Farewells.
Minnesota: Llewellyn Publications.

Masters, Dr. Paul Leon 1978
Rites of the metaphysical Ministry
University of Metaphysics

Moore, Thomas. 1994
CARE OF THE SOUL.
New York: Harper Perennial.

Muller, Wayne. 1993

LEGACY OF THE HEART: The Spiritual
Advantages of a Painful Childhood.
New York: Simon and Schuster, Inc.

Rawlings, Maurice, M.D. 1978
BEYOND DEATHS DOOR
New York: Thomas Nelson, Inc.

Rosen, Eliot Jay. 1998
EXPERIENCING THE SOUL: Before Birth,
During Life, After Death.
Carlsbad, California: Hay House, Inc.

CLOSING THOUGHTS
BY SHARON GILL OESTER

The purpose of my thesis was to relate the hardships that people must endure after losing a loved one or sustaining a devastating loss. This truly has not been a subject given much attention, though there are those professionals who are now realizing the importance of bringing death and grieving to a place where it is evaluated and openly discussed.

The general population has little knowledge of what to expect and thinks that preparing for death is having life insurance and a Will made out. These are just the beginning steps taken to assure that our possessions are allocated and that the survivor is financially secure. These steps in no way prepare us for the grieving process of loss.

Understanding and preparing for the inevitable death of those we love, is working on a spiritual and emotional level. It is nothing that can be bought, it takes teaching and understanding, which at this point in time is very necessary. Little work has been done in an area that effects every one of us. By coming to an understanding of what we can do to prepare ourselves emotionally and spiritually on a daily basis, grief will not hit like a hard blow to the face.

We identify ourselves so fully by our body and our mind that we have forgotten the essence of who we are. We focus on the physical appearance most of all, that is who we are with even our minds and intelligence becoming secondary to the importance of what we look like. Vanity surpasses the value of what, as humans, we can contribute to knowledge and understanding in this life.

Yet the soul, the essence of who we are, is the same essence as that of God. God of All is love, joy and peace. We should seek the things which are our true nature. The things that fill us with the bliss that we are all struggling to find. By identifying ourselves with our soul, we can experience divine light and love within ourselves and the external way we appear would become secondary. Beauty fades away, but the essence of who we are is eternal.

By acknowledging our own mortality, and the death of our physical bodies, no longer will we harbor the fear that death holds for us. The soul does not die; it lives on as can be experienced through meditation. If we seek to find the answers to dispel our fears, we will find them.

Our soul cannot enter into the spiritual realms until it is freed of all negative thought. Meditation requires full, concentrated focus. With the knowledge we gain of what lies beyond this physical life, we can find comfort and strength and help others to find the same understanding.

The answers are there to access, we only have to desire accessing them and learning of what is to come. By understanding death, we prepare ourselves to accept and work through the emotional upheaval we face as survivors and lose the fears of the unknown when our turn comes to leave this plane of existence, we can then fully accept life.

If we come to a deep understanding of the soul, we also come to an understanding of what the souls unmet needs cause within us in life. We also come to understand that it is the soul in us that surpasses physical death. We can learn the importance of loving unconditionally and working through the negative emotions of anger, hate, and resentment and the dangers of holding on to them. We must learn to let these emotions go and learn the practice of forgiving, returning to loving each other in this life.

We have gotten away from the knowledge of our spiritual selves. In a day of high technology, we are constantly distracted by television, radio, computers and other man-made means of taking us from a place of silence within ourselves.

By taking time to know the spiritual beings that we are, listening to our inner voices and gaining knowledge from within ourselves, we will find our lives are more meaningful and more fulfilled. As things are now, we pull farther and farther away from our spirituality and understand less and less of who we are and the abilities we have been given. We have found that the essential things in life are not the material possessions we own. We cannot take those possessions into another plane of existence with us. The truly important things in life are recognizing the spiritual beings that we are and reaching out to help others in their darkest hours.

What we do in life, what we feel in life and the lessons we learn and use in life are what we take with us to the other side of life. We will experience a panoramic life review when we pass on to the spiritual realm and we will be the judges of our own conduct on this physical plane. This knowledge is not new, it has just been forgotten.

ABOUT THE AUTHOR

Dave Oester, DD., Ph.D., and Reiki Master is an ordain and licensed metaphysical minister focusing on the eternal nature of the Afterlife. Dr. Oester has worn many hats in his life. He owned an oil drilling company, worked as a treasure hunter, accountant, paralegal, and as the head of the International Ghost Hunters Society since 1996. He operates a small book publishing business called Coyote Moon Publishing. He has been writing books since 1992. Visit his web site at www.ghostweb.com. He now has thirty-eight nonfiction books and thirteen novels published. You can contact him at ghostsweb@ghotweb.com.